PRAISE FOR
TAKING UP SPACE

Karen's key components of leadership—transparency and communication—are crucial for success on a personal and an organizational level. She lays the foundations of those concepts out beautifully here, in a way that readers can access and apply to their own situations.

—**Marc Casper,** Chairman, President, and CEO,
Thermo Fisher Scientific

Karen is a dynamic leader: direct, decisive, and deeply caring. These traits shine through in *Taking Up Space*, an expert road map to transformational leadership. She models for others, regardless of industry, how to bring authenticity and integrity to the front and create an equitable workplace in which others have the space and support to grow.

—**Jane Fraser,** CEO, Citi

With courage, grace, and the gift of a born teacher and storyteller, Karen delivers a critical message for our current moment—that inspirational leaders need to understand the power of humanizing their roles and focusing on what matters most: people, empathy, communication, and transparency. A leadership manual for our times and a moving and compelling read.

—**Arianna Huffington,** Founder and CEO, Thrive Global

Karen Lynch is a true American success story, who has combined an empathetic, engaging personality with a strong work ethic to become the CEO of CVS Health. In *Taking Up Space* she provides powerful and clear tips for anybody who wants to be successful in the business world, or any professional pursuit.

—**Jonathan Kraft,** President, The Kraft Group,
and President, The New England Patriots

Through her inspiring story of setbacks and triumphs, Karen Lynch re-envisions the future of work to include a greater diversity of people and ideas. *Taking Up Space* is a clear and compelling call to action for all of us and a great reminder that investing in self-leadership, and encouraging others to do the same, can be a truly powerful thing.

—**Hans Vestberg,** Chairman and CEO, Verizon

TAKING UP SPACE

TAKING UP SPACE

Get Heard,
Deliver Results,
and Make a
Difference

KAREN S. LYNCH
President and CEO of CVS Health

1 2 3 4 5 6 7 8 9   LCR   28 27 26 25 24

ISBN   978-1-264-27748-3
MHID   1-264-27748-2

e-ISBN   978-1-264-27749-0
e-MHID   1-264-27749-0

Library of Congress Cataloging-in-Publication Data

Names: Lynch, Karen S., author.
Title: Taking up space : get heard, deliver results, and make a difference / Karen Lynch.
Description: New York : McGraw Hill, [2024] | Includes bibliographical references and index.
Identifiers: LCCN 2023036883 (print) | LCCN 2023036884 (ebook) | ISBN 9781264277483 (hardback) | ISBN 9781264277490 (ebook)
Subjects: LCSH: Lynch, Karen S., author. | Women chief executive officers—United States—Biography. | Health services administrators—United States—Biography. | Success in business—United States.
Classification: LCC HC102.5.L96 A3 2024 (print) | LCC HC102.5.L96 (ebook) | DDC 338.092 [B]—dc23/eng/20230809
LC record available at https://lccn.loc.gov/2023036883
LC ebook record available at https://lccn.loc.gov/2023036884

McGraw Hill books are available at special quantity discounts to use as premiums and sales promotions or for use in corporate training programs. To contact a representative, please visit the Contact Us pages at www.mhprofessional.com.

McGraw Hill is committed to making our products accessible to all learners. To learn more about the available support and accommodations we offer, please contact us at accessibility@mheducation.com. We also participate in the Access Text Network (www.accesstext.org), and ATN members may submit requests through ATN.

To my husband, Kevin, who has always stood by me, supported me through challenging times, and continually encouraged me to take up space.

In memory of Aunt Millie—her lessons and love made all the difference.

In memory of my mother, Irene, whose struggles make me stronger every day.

CONTENTS

INTRODUCTION

If someone had asked me what my career goal was in high school or college, I probably would not have answered "CEO of one of the top 10 largest companies in the US." At that time, in the late 1970s and early 1980s, there was a specific kind of individual who was considered to be leadership material and, as a result, able to access broad professional opportunities. And those individuals didn't look like me or have my background. I worked hard throughout college, balancing school and a part-time job. After college, I earned a series of jobs in the business field and worked diligently to deliver on my professional commitments. All qualities we're told will help us advance in our careers. And yet, after building on many years of professional experience, I was told I didn't fit the profile when I was being considered for a senior executive role at a large company. I didn't look or sound the part. I was specifically told, "You're short, you're petite, you're blonde, your voice isn't deep enough, and you wear too much pink."

By then, I was a seasoned professional with a proven track record of delivering results and demonstrating leadership in various capacities on my résumé. And yet, some still thought I wasn't good enough because of how I looked, how I sounded, and what I wore? As I began writing this book, I thought about my career and the other people who don't fit conventional business profiles and are too often passed over during their career paths. I also thought about what bypassing people who didn't fit a predetermined mold meant for businesses. What are we missing out on? A large pool of talented people with diverse backgrounds, educations, and experiences— something all companies desperately need.

Ultimately, I got that job but could not get the criticism out of my mind. It wasn't that my ego was shattered; rather, it was a stinging reminder that many still cling to old notions about who does and does not fit in or look the part, or who should be allowed to take up space.

When I was a mid-level manager at one company, I was invited to a meeting with the senior managers in my division. I had been at this company for a number of years, coming in early and leaving late, keeping my head down, and putting long hours in each day. I believed that outperforming my objectives would get me noticed and lead to the next opportunity and step in my career. I was so excited when my supervisor asked me to join an important meeting with the senior managers to discuss an upcoming financial transaction. I remember my heart racing as I held the transaction files, notepad, and pen as I tried to calmly walk down to the conference at the end of the hall. I had never been in this executive conference room nor in the presence of these divisional leaders. Thoughts raced through my head as I was trying to anticipate what questions would come up and whether I might be asked to answer or provide details. As I entered the room, I asked one of the leaders in the room where I should sit. He barely glanced at me and told me to "sit in the back, not at the table, because women just take up space."

It's time for those who don't fit the mold and don't want to conform to outdated notions to take up space and create space for others. That's one of the reasons I wrote this book. Not just to tell my story to inspire others to lead differently, but to offer some ways I have overcome the barriers, used my voice, and created opportunities to make a difference.

I chose healthcare for personal and professional reasons, but whatever direction you are passionate about and choose, you have an opportunity to create workplace environments where a variety of voices can be heard and appreciated. Some of you may be in leadership positions but want to do more. This book is for you. You may have already mapped out what kind of difference you want to make and are working toward it but wish you could be more effective. This book is for you. You may not be sure where you want to go, but you'd like ideas for ways to get there once you figure it out. This book is for you. Your own vision of what you want to do and how you want to do it may shift. Your current plans may not play out as you expected. That's OK. This book is for you too.

The path for you won't be linear (mine wasn't) or entirely predictable (ditto!). That's OK. Detours will come on the horizon. Life will take different curves. It's what you do with the twists and turns that matters.

Until now, I would never have shared anything about my personal story with business colleagues, let alone the public. Instead, I would just describe myself as the plainest person you'll ever meet: Karen Jones, from East Street in the small western Massachusetts town of Ware, an old mill town founded in 1717 with a population of just over 10,000. Now I know my story can become part of the conversation around taking up space and creating it for others, and perhaps inspire those who have felt unheard and ignored. As you read my story for overcoming systemic obstacles facing too many of us, understand that you have the power to gain the influence and voice you deserve. And in that process, you will help evolve companies to be and do better. It's in your hands.

Thank you for allowing me to share my story with you—and if you have a moment, I would love to hear yours. Contact me at KarenSLynch.com.

The Girl from (Any)Ware: Strength Through Vulnerability

Our histories shape who we are but do not determine the person we become.

It was like I had been shoved down a steep, endless, dark chute. My stomach was in my throat. My head pounded; my brain burst with a million jumbled thoughts. I remember hearing someone talking, but it seemed like a string of nonsense that had no meaning after those first few potent words had been delivered—*your mother is gone.*

I was just 12 when my mother died by suicide at age 42. Even though she had been ill for many years, the idea that I would lose her forever was not something my young mind had ever contemplated. She had schizophrenia, and because of that, my three siblings and I had become accustomed to a life quite different from anyone else we knew. We always had a certain amount of shame and humiliation around our mother. She was an ICU nurse at Massachusetts General Hospital and a highly educated woman, but her illness made it difficult for her to lead a normal life or for us to have conventional childhoods. I remember her saying odd, random things. "Dumb are men" is one memorable line she would utter at the most unlikely and, for an adolescent, embarrassing times. And then there were her long walks that would often last for hours before she returned home with little recollection of where she had been or what she had done, at least in terms of what she could communicate to us.

My 16-year-old sister Cheryl (four years older than me) and I had come home from an unremarkable day at school. I was excited, however, because this was the day I would get a pair of long-coveted Earth Shoes, utilitarian-looking brown leather slip-on shoes that were all the rage among my classmates. It was one of the few times I would get something "everyone else" had, and the antic-ipation rushed through me. We said hello and called for our mother as usual, but there was no reply. Cheryl found her first and pushed me out of the way so I wouldn't see. I wasn't sure of what was happening, and I don't remember much after that, except a great deal of commotion and someone telling me what had happened in the most per-functory way possible, or at least it seemed to me in the confusion. Just like that.

Almost immediately after my mother died, I went to stay with a close friend. My siblings found similar accommodations. After a few days of being with my friend and her family, we went to stay with our Aunt Millie, my mother's sister, who lived two doors over from my house, in the same classic New England four-plex where we had lived with our mom. Millie was also a single mother, a widow with a son of her own. She became my mentor and role model and the strongest person I knew.

Ideas about my future might have been stifled if not for my Aunt Millie. As soon as she was old enough, probably 16 or 17, she took a job at the Carter's, Inc. clothing factory in Springfield, Massachusetts, and stayed there until she became too sick to work in her late fifties. During those working years, she had gotten married and had a son. Her husband passed away early in their marriage, and she took on the role of sole breadwinner and caretaker of her only son. When her parents, who had immigrated from Poland, were ailing, she took care of them too. After my mother died, she added on the responsibility of raising her sister's four children, including me, without hesitation.

She was a strong woman who didn't let anything get in the way of raising her family and providing for them. That perspective helped form many of my defining values: a sense of duty, personal responsibility, integrity, honesty, and stick-to-itiveness. Much of Millie's philosophy was grounded in being an immigrant to a strange country where she had to prove herself, and some came from her economic circumstances, which were meager. "You have no choice, keep moving forward, don't quit, don't give up" are all Millie-isms I learned living with and watching my aunt work hard and give back to her community. I remember her saying to me once, "I want you to know I love you, but I don't get close to people because you lose them." I had no doubt she loved me very much, and I adopted her sentiment. The distance I kept from other people while my mother was alive widened after she died. My aunt's philosophy only reinforced my need to create emotional chasms. I shut down almost completely after my mother died. The idea of sharing my feelings with anyone, even my own family, petrified me. I believed that if I showed any vulnerability at all, the tears would start again and never stop.

When I started high school, I became an Honor Roll hellion. I aced my classes with high marks. I was a cheerleader. But I would also go out drinking quite often. I smoked pot to medicate myself from the pain I refused to talk about, even to myself. It was a teenage indulgence I gave up before I graduated. But "it"—my mother's death—was never far from the surface. One day after school, I drove around town with a group of friends. I didn't know all the people in the car, and they didn't know me. As we drove past my apartment, one passenger pointed at the building and said, "That's the house where the woman hung herself." That's how people talked about what happened, as trivial gossip. I remained quiet; friends who knew about my mom hid their mortification with an embarrassed silence.

Millie was stoic, and I followed her lead. Coming and going to school from Aunt Millie's apartment every day, I lived in the same building where my mother had died, and that was hard for a young girl, but Aunt Millie demonstrated to me what resilience looked like. If she could manage being a widow, showing up to a laborious job, raising her son, raising my siblings and me, and still putting food on the table every night, I could manage the walk to and from home every day.

She also taught me the value of hard work and doing whatever job you had as best you could. This is such an important lesson since it related to the big concepts we continue to talk about today: humility, pride, and entitlement. There is no job that is not worth doing well or feeling proud of for having done it well, no job that is beneath us, and no reason we are entitled to a job we have not earned. When I was in high school, I worked at a local Western Massachusetts grocery store chain called Big Y. I wanted to be the best cashier ever, so every day I worked, I would go in with the attitude of wanting to beat my numbers from the day before. This was before scanning machines; you had to put the numbers into the cash register manually. I also had to do a great deal of math in my head. I generally beat out the previous day's numbers, and it made a generally tedious job more interesting. My competitive spirit (even if it was just with myself) can be attributed to Aunt Millie.

Millie was also practical. She was wise with her money and told us never to depend on someone else. That was a big deal for me, a lesson I took to heart. We were frugal because we had to be, but I still understand the value of being careful with money. I confess to using coupons! When I went off to college, she told me not to come home until Thanksgiving, knowing that it would be better for me financially and socially to stay on campus for as long as possible. At that point, my oldest brother, Jimmy, was out of the house and living outside of Boston, and I lived with him on college breaks during summers when I was working on Cape Cod, and he'd rent a house with some friends. He gave me my first car and taught me how to drive a stick shift—he even showed me how to throw a football the right way.

But frugality is not the same as stinginess, and generosity was another behavior Millie modeled for us that has become important to my life as a person and as a leader. Her involvement in the community instilled in us the idea of giving back and helping others. She did so much for so many over her lifetime, helping to establish a community center in Ware, delivering meals to people in need, and helping individual neighbors and friends whenever and however she could—raising us would have been enough, but for Millie, it wasn't. There was always another way to reach out and help. I strive to exemplify this in my professional roles but also personally too when it is right to do so: paying for the groceries for people behind me in line or telling a waitress in a restaurant that I want to take care of a family's bill at a nearby table, always quickly walking out the door. I do this for Millie. Small acts can have a big ripple effect. You really can change the world with kindness and caring.

I was in my early twenties when Millie became ill with emphysema and breast and lung cancer. Seeing her so ill and trying to help navigate the hospital and medical system made me acutely aware of the shortcomings of the healthcare industry. Her eventual passing brought back much of the pain and uncertainty I felt when I lost my mother. Another anchor, gone. My mother's death fostered a desire to improve mental health awareness and treatment; losing Aunt Millie in such an untimely and cruel way committed me to do whatever I could to improve how we access healthcare.

Many of us have experienced trauma, loss, and pain. These deep emotional experiences shape our lives and behaviors. We become conscious of how our past affects our present, but we must also take the reins to respond to our past in ways that reshape the future—our own, and the world's.

As a consequence of the losses I experienced as a child and young adult, and taking a cue from Aunt Millie's stoicism, I kept a distance from people well into adulthood. I would succumb to a nonemotional place, putting on blinders and building walls, personally and professionally. I did have friends and relationships, of course, but I admit they never got much below the surface of feelings and emotions. I was always good at numbers—they put the world in order. One day in high school, an accountant guest speaker came to one of my math classes and discussed accounting. As I listened, I thought, yeah, I can do that. I could excel in it and make a pretty good living. One of my teachers in high school supported me in this goal, shepherding me through career day and a visit to Boston College, where I enrolled and graduated with a degree in accounting. That was so helpful, but it was not a relationship I nurtured, and I probably should have. I didn't know how.

When applying to college, I remember thinking, "Karen, make sure you study a technical skill because it will carry you somewhere, no matter what." Millie's practicality! Once I had enrolled at BC, I didn't receive much professional guidance, but somehow, I made my way into public accounting, even before clearly understanding what it was. Astonishing as it sounds, accounting became a kind of refuge for me. I was good at it and working with numbers was satisfying: they are orderly and predictable. For someone who grew up surrounded by chaos and uncertainty, the controlled precision of accounting was beautiful.

THE PAST AND YOUR PURPOSE

My aunt's death hit me hard; a second mother, gone forever. Losing my mother and aunt at such a young age taught me that through the most painful times in our lives, we often discover our strength and purpose. It was after my aunt died that I made the decision to dedicate my life and career to the pursuit of better, more accessible healthcare that was also inclusive of mental health. Ironically, what motivated me the most was the sense of frustration and helplessness I felt while caring for my aunt. Trying to navigate a confusing and complicated healthcare system effectively was challenging. I didn't know what questions to ask the doctors let alone if it was even appropriate to approach them with my concerns and fears. Doctors were authority figures who didn't openly encourage many questions, especially from young women. Worse, I had no clue how to respond when my aunt was in pain. Instinctively, I knew that it wasn't just her physical hurt that needed to be addressed but her emotional anguish as well. But how? Not knowing what to do or where to go was a terrible feeling.

After she passed, I wanted to do whatever I could to prevent others from experiencing the same inadequate care she and my mother had fallen victim to. These deeply personal and heart-wrenching experiences remain central drivers of my long-time passion for transforming all levels of healthcare to treat the whole person, not just the patient, throughout their entire health journey. Health is more than just about our physical condition. Our mental health and other factors like behavior and environment greatly influence our well-being. To treat health effectively and comprehensively, we need to provide whole-person care.

My own heartbreak at losing the people closest to me held me back in many ways, and I share the insight I gained from realizing and working to overcome it—a great part of this work involved empathy and caring. For a long time, I didn't want to tell people about why my mother died, terrified they would hold it against me or, worse, that they would think I had some affliction that would prevent me from being an effective executive. But I've changed. I now feel obligated to share what I've learned about the power that comes from vulnerability, empathy, and authenticity, things not taught in any business course I know of but essential for anyone who wants to lead.

It's vital that leaders understand the value of humanizing their roles. Considering what we experienced during the COVID-19 pandemic over the last several years, it's particularly important. Most of us have realized that clear communication and compassion are as important as supply chains and revenue-generating businesses. As someone who spent many years holding other people at arm's length, I can tell you it doesn't work if you want to lead and make a difference today and in the future. Leaders of all kinds have to connect authentically with their colleagues, customers, and constituents if they want their organizations to thrive and become meaningful partners of the communities they serve. It's not easy, I get it. But it is absolutely nonnegotiable for anyone wanting to stay the course, realize their potential, and transform businesses.

Looking back to where I had come from and where I am now was a humbling experience. There's an idea that anyone from anywhere can make it in America, but I am not sure how many people really believe that. So many doors continue to remain closed to too many people. That's starting to change, but when I was growing up, there were people in Ware who believed that my siblings and I wouldn't amount to anything, given our background and the tragedy that had befallen us. We were from the wrong side of the tracks, with no pedigree or distinction. My father left the family when I was too young to remember him, and I had a single mother before "single mother" was a familiar term (and not a pejorative). In January 2015, the local paper, the *Ware River News,* asked me to write a letter about my promotion after I was named president of Aetna, the managed healthcare company. Composing the note took a few minutes, but I savored writing it.

Despite my mother being a highly qualified nurse, as a consequence of being in a one-parent household and the fact that she was ill for a good part of the time I was a little girl, we were barely middle class. Overcoming skepticism from others was one of the many challenges I faced growing up, and it helped shape who I am today. Part of the pleasure in writing that note to the newspaper came from the thought that a young person might read it and be inspired: There are so many possibilities. There is a world beyond your doorstep. Don't limit your thinking for any reason, especially because of your background.

REMEMBER THIS:

▶ **Your past does not determine your future.** There is a world beyond your doorstep. Don't limit your thinking because of where you're from or how you grew up, or even because of past missteps. Correct mistakes, live for today, and keep your eyes trained on the future.

▶ **Resilience and optimism are a powerful combination.** The ability to stay the course when things are tough is made easier through a positive attitude. It's not just an old saying—the best and most effective leaders see the upside in even difficult situations, enabling them to stay the course and recover from setbacks more quickly.

▶ **Setbacks are not life sentences.** Don't let a devastating situation or any setback prevent you from reaching your goals.

2

Own Your Past to Define a Better Future

Find purpose through the power of care.

s I look back on my formative years, so much of what I carry with me today as a leader, I learned from Millie. So much of what inspired me to enter my field is also thanks to her. From my very first accounting job at Ernst & Whinney (now Ernst & Young) in my early twenties, I managed my working life from the point of view of getting things done. Productivity kept me busy and distracted—mostly from my own emotions.

During my final year in college, Ernst & Whinney (EW) in Boston offered me a job on the spot after I had gone for a senior-year interview. To this day, I vividly remember taking the Metrorail, known in Boston as the "T," from downtown and then running from the stop to my friend's apartment to announce to her, "I got a job!" I was so excited because I felt strongly that I had to figure out my life very quickly, and this job would immediately start me on a clear path.

I was also petrified. I knew nothing about the business world. The first day in the office felt like I had been expelled to a foreign country. The EW offices were traditional and formal, in keeping with both its history and the business of accounting, which must instill trust and a sense of stability in clients. From then on, I had two lives, work and home, which were completely different. My tiny one-bedroom rental apartment in a duplex in central Massachusetts was $325 a month. It was basic, drab, and functional. I had no time, money, or understanding of how to decorate what I thought of as a temporary way station. The lessons in frugality I learned from Aunt Millie helped me stick to a budget and pay my bills.

I remember the noise from a couple with a baby in the apartment below me who would fight constantly. I could not take their arguing, it was sad and disturbing. So I would work late, hoping that when I arrived home, they wouldn't be around. Eventually, I moved into an apartment in Worcester with my best friend from high school. I took a Peter Pan bus into Boston daily because I had no reliable car.

After the EW training program, I was placed on my first audit, which is an official accounting of a company's financials. I accompanied one of the partners on these jobs, which helped me understand corporate accounting and become more familiar with the rhythm of work and office life.

It was a big moment and a huge relief when I finally passed all my CPA exams. Like many, I had failed the exams the first two times but was undeterred. They are difficult, and I would not let myself get weeded out, so I hit the books to study much more aggressively before giving myself another chance to pass them. A few weeks after taking the tests for the third time, I went to the mailbox and saw the envelope. "Oh God, the grades are here," I thought. The slim white packet sat on my lap for some time before I worked up the courage to open it. "Maybe," I thought, "if it sits here long enough, the grades will all turn to passing." I guess it worked because I passed all four tests. It was a huge relief because acing the tests is the most critical step in continuing to practice public accounting. I had taken my Aunt Millie's advice, never give up, and it had paid off.

I stayed at the firm for nearly five years, specializing in insurance. But I wanted to broaden myself, which meant finding a job outside public accounting. I had also gone back home to Western Massachusetts to be with my Aunt Millie, who was ill with cancer, and it was during that time I experienced some of the frustrations of the healthcare system that would later become my life's mission to address. Sitting at her bedside in the hospital, I felt helpless, not knowing what to ask or how to advocate for her. It was then that I made a commitment to myself that somehow I would try to make a difference in healthcare.

My work was being noticed in the industry, which means that people pay attention to who is doing what in all industries because smart companies always search for talented individuals. Even if you don't think anyone is paying attention to your efforts, they are. As a case in point, an executive from a globally managed health insurance company recruited me just months later. He is still a dear friend and important mentor. I later came across his notes for my job interview with him. He said I had energy and passion but that I thought I was more experienced than I actually was. I don't remember feeling that way, but it was an impression that likely came from my natural distance. Friendly but emotionally aloof, I probably left some people with the impression that I believed I was more experienced than I really was. The company was supportive, and I took on the job as a health plan accounting leader, with several accountants from half the country reporting to me. In retrospect, the job may have been more involved than what I was ready for, but I applied focus and did it. I didn't have time to make many new friends in this position because I was learning and doing the job simultaneously, and I didn't want to screw it up.

I learned a great deal at this company in the 18 years I was there. I discovered that one of my strengths is talking to customers; I love understanding how people experience products and how I can make that experience better. If I hadn't learned this about myself, I might have made very different decisions about my career. Understanding how to grow business sectors, along with distribution and sales, was very useful. I learned quite a lot about the sales side of the business in that role, which was invaluable because it's so much about relationships and building working connections, customer retention, and growth.

I took on a number of roles—including president of the group employer disability, dental, and vision care businesses—that allowed me to understand many aspects of the insurance industry.

When I looked at insurance, I didn't see it through the lens of risk assessment; I looked at it through a customer's eyes. There is only so much you can know about insurance through the numbers. What drove me was that the core of my responsibilities was caring for people— helping them improve their health, lowering costs, and navigating a sometimes inscrutable system. I also wanted internal teams to understand the experience for our customers when they use their insurance benefits and access the care they needed.

Executives may not be able to try every job in a company, but they should at least understand every job. I was not shy about bringing in outside people to help me with aspects of the work I didn't understand well enough to manage independently. But the irony of that was I was still very closed-off personally. I stubbornly kept to my policy of not revealing the inner Karen. It was much easier for me to show concern for others without sharing my own vulnerabilities, although, in retrospect, doing so would have made me an even more effective manager.

Meanwhile, I watched colleagues form lasting friendships that helped them as their careers grew and expanded. I am sure an emotional component of these relationships brought them a sense of satisfaction from spending a good deal of their lives in the office. Going out for dinner and drinks after work to unwind with colleagues was unimportant to me, although looking back on it now, I can see value in it for many people—even maybe me. It can help to forge stronger relationships and camaraderie. I kept my blinders on, focusing on the job before me. My aunt reassured me that she loved me but wouldn't always demonstrate it emotionally. That stayed with me for a long time. That became my modus operandi, too—and my fear. I did have a handful of friends, of course, but they, too, were kept at a safe distance. After several years of friendship, one friend was surprised to learn that I had siblings because I had never mentioned them. Even one of my administrative assistants didn't know I had a family, and we had worked together for many years.

As I rose up the ladder professionally in a male-dominated environment where you do not share feelings, my emotional armor weighed heavier. This insight struck me sharply at one point during my time at this job, and I realized that sometimes the greatest responsibility you have is to yourself. There came one of those moments when I had to stop and think hard about what I was doing and why. I had been working endless hours for months on divestitures and was physically and mentally exhausted. Right after completing that project, I was asked to take on another big assignment, and I could not accept it. I was burned out. In addition, at the time, my aunt was sick, and I felt that I really needed to be by her side in Western Massachusetts. So I made the difficult decision to leave this company and take a job that was much closer to my family. Perhaps a long vacation or family leave would have been the better remedy for how I felt, but I was burned out. I'd had it. Quitting seemed to be the only option, so that is what I did, even though the chief financial officer (CFO), who was both a mentor and a sponsor to me, advised me that I was making the wrong decision. When I left, he told me I'd return in six months. When you change jobs, you should go to something, not run from something.

Once I was back in Massachusetts, I accepted a position at another insurance company. This remains the biggest mistake of my career. I didn't like the job or the company; it was not the right culture or environment for me. I could not be as effective as I would have been if I had enjoyed the environment and the work. I was there for about a year and was looking for another job for half that time. This was an important lesson: not all corporate cultures work for all people. Don't feel you have failed because the fit isn't right.

It is ironic that I left the other company because I was overstressed from a bad case of burnout, but my new situation only added more stress. Fortunately, the CFO of my previous company reached out to me at the right moment (he knew better than I did that this company was not going to work out) and asked if I was ready to come back. I sure was. I returned to the company as its healthcare financial controller. I remain forever grateful to my mentor for continuing to believe in me, despite the fact I had quit.

The worst time to make a career-changing decision— or any decision of consequence—is when you are burnt out or under tremendous pressure. I learned through painful experience that my analytical skills and ability to reason were not functioning as they should have been when I was mentally tired and physically exhausted. The best thing to have done was to have taken some time off. I know better now. And I urge anyone in a similar situation to request time to regroup. Most companies that value their people will grant such time.

I learned that to be a change-maker, you must challenge the existing system if it is not working, speak up, and ask for what you need, something I wish I had been more forceful about early in my career. If you challenge things that are not working for you or are not in the best interests of your employees and your business with sincerity and respect, you can make yourself heard—and people will listen. I remember once being at an after-hours business meeting, and the people around the table (junior- and mid-management-level colleagues, including myself) being asked what they would be doing had they not been at this meeting. Most said they would be working or studying to take their actuarial exams, but I said, "I'd be at my aerobics class, so this better be good." The late Jim Stewart, who was running the meeting, saw something in me with that one exchange. He told me he'd keep an eye on my career, which he did in many helpful ways. I learned that being honest and direct is never bad advice.

TIME HEALS SOME WOUNDS

It would be decades before I felt comfortable talking about my childhood and my mother's mental illness

with coworkers, supervisors, and other colleagues—
even friends. I was embarrassed. Ashamed. Frightened.
As a woman with ambitions and also one who was determined to support myself, I believed that if I showed any
vulnerability at all, people would take advantage of it—
especially in a business setting, where these fears are
not unfounded. Because mental illness had (and still
has) a profound stigma attached to it, and because it is
so misunderstood, even by educated people, there was a
good chance that at certain times during my career, my
history could have been used against me. *What if it happens to her? Is there something wrong with her? Maybe we
shouldn't invest in her?*

As I gained experience, my insight into insurance,
hospitals, doctors, and all the other players in the healthcare industry expanded, and I started to form a vision for
a more holistic, consumer-centric approach to health. So
why was I hiding information about myself that could
help change hearts and minds, not to mention policies
and procedures when it came to healthcare? I remem-
bered sitting in my aunt's hospital room when she was
sick, not knowing what questions to ask the doctors. I
didn't know what to do to care for her. I never want anyone else to go through that. Telling my story would be
important in motivating others to help create a more
local, simple, personalized, and holistic system. I could
only be a part of that transformation if I were willing to
open myself up.

More importantly, by being unwilling to lift the mask,
I was doing a disservice to myself and the people I was
working with. My definition of professionalism—friendly

but distant, casual but aloof, enthusiastic but shielded—came from my own fears of getting in touch with my pain. Remaining shut off would hurt the people who were counting on me to lead, and it would also hurt me.

Owning up to our personal anxieties, insecurities, histories, or upbringings is an asset, especially when you are around people who can sense inauthenticity. Running and spin classes are good for my body and mind, but embracing the wholeness of who I am was essential for my spirit. I knew that if I was going to lead a large healthcare company and create a truly diverse team of engaged people who felt heard, appreciated, and recognized, I had to become a trusted partner, not just a manager handing out deadlines, orders, and expectations. If I wanted to succeed at an audacious mission to change the way people access health services and medicine, I had to use and share my experiences as the daughter of a woman who had died from suicide and as the niece of a woman who couldn't access the right healthcare when she needed it most. I had to stop running from my core and hiding that part of me from others. I had to take up space. The mask had to come off.

Embracing my past experiences makes my drive to change the system meaningful and more powerful. First, I had to sit with myself and come to terms with where I came from and how I felt about it. It was scary. I worried that if I started to talk about my past, I'd start to cry and have a hard time stopping. Was that a real possibility? Was that the worst that would happen? Would it be so terrible if it did happen? What would crying uncontrollably feel like? It might be messy. It might be hard. It could get ugly. Embarrassing. Painful. But it would also be liberating. Fear and pain are on a pendulum, and on the other side are joy and pleasure. The tears do stop. Once that wave crashes, the water is glorious. I was all in because I had no choice, ultimately, but to start being honest about who I was and how it was part of the work I wanted to do in my career and my life.

VULNERABILITY IS AN ASSET IN LEADERSHIP

I don't define myself only as a CEO. I'm a spouse of a CEO, a grandmother (I prefer "mimsy" to "granny"), a dog mom, and a person with many outside interests, including sports, nature, and music. So I talk about the emotional aspects of good leadership because we have to get real if we're going to make a difference. As I did, many driven, successful people use work as a distraction. It can and does serve you. For a while. When I was building my career, work was my outlet. Even though I knew that I was missing out on the opportunities for personal growth that comes from the camaraderie and collegiality of office life, I was getting things done. My managers noticed. I was climbing the ladder, getting close to the glass ceiling. I had great mentors and teams. Early in my career, my arm's-length approach to human dynamics didn't seem to be a detriment. A mentor used to say to me, "Don't work all the time. Take vacations; I take all of mine. If you don't, you're not that interesting. You need to be interested in other people, and you need to be interesting to others. If you work all the time, it's not interesting." To accomplish big things today, at some point, even successful team builders have to say, "Here are my scrapes, scars, and bruises. I have them too. Here's what I'm interested in outside of work." This attitude helps you to relate to people on a more meaningful level.

Your fears and anxieties may or may not come from childhood or trauma. You might be wearing a mask for other reasons. But I know I'm not alone in this. Studies show that CEOs, founders, innovators, and entrepreneurs are more prone to conditions such as depression and anxiety than other people. Challenging childhoods, tumultuous pasts, insecurities, and disappointment— these can be the driving force of our determination and success. We can be productive and innovative. But we're not using all of our power. Conventional wisdom (or fear) says that being honest about our hardships can isolate us putting our status or position at risk (there was a time when I was right there with you on this one); I now believe it does not.

Everyone who wants to lead a charge, whether a CEO, small business owner, or community volunteer, has to claim who they are and share their humanity with colleagues and customers. It can be hard to do, but you must start small and build confidence over time. Share one thing. Then another when it's relevant to do so. We have so much more to bring to the table from our emotional selves than we are often comfortable with. It's hard. Dropping the mask, taking off the blinders, and knocking down the emotional walls you've built doesn't mean you can't be a strong, decisive leader. On the contrary, I believe remembering and sharing relevant truths about our lives makes us more powerful and effective. It builds trust and loyalty, which is crucial if we intend to change the status quo in our businesses.

Before I could realize progress in the healthcare delivery system, I had to be in a position to take up space and have an impact. While it's true that there isn't one road to making a difference, I was in the corporate world, where I felt confident and prepared.

My mission was twofold: to be in a position that allowed me to make changes, and then to actually create strategies for those changes to be implemented. Most recently, that meant surviving the merger of two large companies, helping to integrate them, and then achieving a position that would give me a meaningful role in shaping how we operate the business to make a bigger impact.

I was only going to make this work if I owned my past, wasn't afraid of it, and was honest about it with myself and others.

Sharing the relevant truths about our lives makes us more powerful and effective.

On December 3, 2017, CVS Health announced it would acquire Aetna for $69 billion, where I had been president since 2015. I stayed on as president of the Aetna business unit, and I became an executive vice president of CVS Health. The megamerger of two companies in the same business but serving different sectors—insurance versus retail pharmacy—was typical in some ways. Primary among them was that very few executives survive such mergers when the dust settles. Of the four most senior executives who stayed,[1] I was the only woman to do so, and I took the opportunity to craft and ask for a role that allowed me to change how people access and benefit from healthcare services.

I was interested in the CVS Health executive vice president job because it would allow me to continue to lead Aetna while also learning more about CVS Health and its operations, including a retail operation like the CVS Pharmacy business, which is vastly different from the complexities of operating an insurance company. Retail operations have to constantly plan for consumers' needs around health and wellness products. This includes ensuring a stable supply chain, inventory, and logistics around distribution centers and transportation. Acute environmental conditions like severe weather and frontline labor shortages affect retail differently than they do other professional service industries like insurance. So, while the two businesses were a natural fit from a consumer health perspective, they didn't fit together naturally. It would be an interesting integration. And at the end of the day, all of the company's moving parts were about delivering healthcare—that's what really mattered to me.

The prospect of staying on gave me pause because I knew most of the senior managers would leave Aetna, some voluntarily and others not. There would be the inevitable redundancy or overlap at the middle and senior management levels, as there often is under these circumstances. Ultimately, I felt responsible for continuing at the company long enough to lead the organization through the integration. Yet remaining at the new company was not guaranteed.

For me, the decision to stay or go represented a crossroads for me professionally and in terms of my life purpose.

THE FAULT LINES

Flashback to 2014, a year before I was named president of Aetna. I was the executive vice president (EVP) of local and regional businesses that represented half the company, and I was in line for a larger role. A consulting firm had been hired to do an executive assessment of my potential. I was in Aetna's succession plan for the CEO role, and this evaluation was part of the process. An executive assessment looks at the strengths and weaknesses of potential leaders. It's a rigorous and confidential engagement, which entails talking anonymously to many—in my case, 16—colleagues, peers, staff, and superiors. There are other assessment systems used that measure leadership competencies, emotional intelligence, nonverbal cognitive ability, and critical thinking.

The results are comprehensive and detailed. My deep knowledge of and expertise in the healthcare sector were duly noted. My leadership style was praised, and I'm very proud of that: "An ability to energize and motivate co-workers, Karen is very customer-focused with strong interpersonal sensitivity and a knack for building talented leadership teams. Karen seeks input from the appropriate talent, creates a blended team, and holds them accountable. Her enthusiasm, empathy, and caring about others create a compelling leadership style that motivates people to trust her and work hard for her and her organization. Comfortable soliciting ideas and opinions from her team and coming to decisions in ambiguous situations, Karen is able to take risks amidst uncertainty. When situations change quickly, Karen has shown the ability to be flexible and nimble in decision-making using the best available data."

It was reassuring, flattering, and immensely satisfying that my skills as a leader were recognized and appreciated. I had always worked hard to be inclusive and care about my entire team, including direct reports, colleagues, or managers. Collaboration, listening skills, and a willingness to go outside of conventional business solutions are hallmarks that I worked hard to build. My leadership style demands high expectations but never asks anyone to do what I would not do myself. I drive accountability by focusing on the customer's point of view. I give people as much latitude as possible but also coach and redirect them when they are not delivering. It was great to see these qualities acknowledged in writing. Great, that is, until the last page of the report. It's all fun and games until you read something that's true but you don't want to see. "Personality-based challenges: May not value the self-reflection needed for personal development."

There it was. That arm's-length philosophy, spelled out in polite management-speak. That don't-get-too-close-or-else part that I thought no one noticed because I was so good at being externally directed and team-spirited. If I was going to turn my passion for holistic healthcare and taking care of the whole person into part of a business model, I needed to take this criticism seriously.

The report was right: if I was going to lead Aetna, I had to do the soul-searching or self-reflection that would enable me to come to terms with who I am.

It would be scary opening up to people—colleagues, friends, customers, strangers—about my mother and my own struggles to overcome that grief. But because my mom died by suicide, I believe very strongly in promoting mental health awareness and making sure people have access to the services that they need. And I would have a chance to do it at Aetna.

During one Aetna town hall in 2016 with 50,000 colleagues in attendance, I finally did. I received a very positive reaction. People were shocked but supportive. It was hard, but afterward, I felt lighter. I know I am not the same little girl who lost her mother. That little girl is part of me but is not the Karen S. Lynch I am today. I love and embrace her for helping shape me. The armor was finally really off.

I have to give my husband, Kevin, a lot of credit for helping me decide to talk about the personal aspects of my past. We discussed using it as a platform, so people feel a connection to me in a different way. It would also give me a powerful point of entry for talking about mental health and how it is an aspect of healthcare often forgotten about or treated as an aside.

It has gotten easier to talk about my mom since. I watch people's reactions, and they often don't know what to say. That's part of the reason I talk about my experience with suicide. We have to be comfortable discussing hard things; it's the only way we can find better solutions to challenges like mental health issues. I am very comfortable with it now. Living in the world is messy, and no one has a perfect life. Talking about myself personally has rounded me out and made me more approachable, which is important as a leader who wants to address big issues in the healthcare industry. I need other people's input, and if they don't feel comfortable around me or if they don't trust me, that's a big problem. Being honest about the past is also honoring who you are. I'm not hiding anything anymore. What a relief!

Even as I worked through the height of the COVID-19 pandemic and held a virtual town hall, I talked about personal things that were relevant to what we were all going through. I shared a story about learning to be a better cook. I was so excited to share a complete meal I had prepared with Kevin and had to laugh when he told me it was great and only lacked one thing: flavor. The response I received from team members was amazingly positive. I also started to learn Polish, an important connection with my heritage—which turned out to be a more successful endeavor than my cooking. People like to hear about the human side of others, especially leaders.

I learned many coping skills through trial and error. The resilience I developed, thanks to my aunt, and the optimism I practice that has helped make the pain of my loss more manageable have been absolutely crucial to my success and survival in the competitive and male-dominated, traditional fields of accounting and insurance. But it was when I finally said to the world, "This is me, Karen S. Lynch, daughter, niece, sister, hurt little girl, scared young woman, fearless dreamer, and doer," that I was able to look at my past in the eye.

My vulnerabilities, and yours, are signs of strength. Yes, I know it is hard to reveal what has traditionally been viewed as weakness, as cracks to be opened and exploited. But it is wrong to think exposing our vulnerability undermines our executive strength, expertise, or even our authority. Have the confidence to leverage your experiences, even the painful ones, and put them to the test. We are in a moment when people—colleagues, constituents, and customers—are hungry to see leaders as people and to know they relate to their fears and pain points because they've been there themselves and have demonstrated a way to overcome them. Being vulnerable puts you out there and makes you more transparent, which makes you more accountable to your promise to enable the authenticity of your team.

ENJOY THE RIDE

Anytime I get a promotion or accolade, my husband, Kevin, gives me a card that says "How plain are you now, Jonesy?" Charming and loving, it's also a profound reminder that our futures are not set in stone. We don't have to be who we were yesterday, if that person isn't serving us. Life events inform us, but they don't define us, and they don't prescribe our destinies. My history and my response to it are mine. I own it. But it does not own me.

Drawing on my unconventional business journey, I share what I believe to be the most important qualities you need to lead strong and transformative companies today and into the future: accountability, vulnerability, authenticity, integrity, equity in all things (health access, pay, etc.), strategic risk, active listening, inclusion, and genuine diversity. These are themes that run through this book because they are intrinsic to taking up space. We must understand how to assess and claim our value, cracks and all. But I also believe in being a strong self-advocate. You need to be open to the insights and lessons you learn that help shape how you lead throughout your career journey.

There are so many dynamics at work in business now, including a legitimate demand for greater social consciousness and accountability on the part of executives or leaders of any kind. The accountability starts with us—with our hearts and our minds.

REMEMBER THIS:

► **People are watching and learning from you even when it may not seem to be the case.** The way you present yourself to others, the way you work and take responsibility, is noticed by those around you and within your industry. Be truthful and responsible always, especially during challenging times, because the payoff is the respect of others—and self-respect.

► **Let your cracks show.** Sharing your personal vulnerabilities is a sign of strength and makes you a more relatable and effective manager. Being open allows for transformation and growth, professionally and personally. Vulnerability is an asset that can transform a manager to a leader. Your truth honors who you are.

► **Acknowledge the pain points of others.** We are in a moment when our stakeholders are hungry to see us as people and to know we truly relate to their fears and challenges because we've been there.

3

Emotional Baggage Will Weigh You Down

Talk openly about what everyone is thinking about but is avoiding—put the moose on the table.

remember standing up in my high school World History class, overcome with frustration, and announcing, "This is the most boring class I've ever been in." I was frustrated that this dry topic was not relevant to anything that was happening in our lives today. I was voicing what many classmates felt but did not dare say. The teacher, Peter Baltren, not only didn't toss me out of class and into the principal's office, he actually engaged in a conversation about my frustration. He stressed the importance of having the courage to raise the tough issues. After that outburst, sometime later, he guided me into considering Boston College. Even back then, I put the moose on the table, an expression I learned from an executive workshop I attended several years later, which was inspired in part by a book by the same name by Randall Tobias. Talk about the hard things, and admit out loud what everyone else is thinking about. In this case, the recipient of that moose took me under his wing. Later in my career, his daughter told me that her dad had watched my career and was proud of me. I am so grateful for Mr. Baltren's tolerance of my outburst and subsequent guidance, including his advice to go to Boston College. It was a good decision for me because it was the right size school for me and offered me a good financial aid package (which I needed—Aunt Millie's pragmatism was and is always with me). He made me see that the education BC offered could help me go where I wanted to go. I really don't think BC would have happened had I not put the moose on the table that day in World History. Are you willing to take a chance and say what is on your mind? I hope you are, but consider being a bit more tactful than I was.

If you want a voice that commands respectful attention, you have to know how to have difficult and uncomfortable conversations in a way that does not alienate people. This takes practice for most of us. Effective advocacy for yourself or your ideas, opinions, and requests starts with making your arguments clear and understandable. The last thing you want to do is put people on the defensive—which may have been the case with Mr. Baltren, had he not been an experienced and open-minded teacher. But the alternative—not saying what needs to be said—can result in festering resentment, which affects your morale and the morale of those around you if you allow it to spill over into your attitude. This sounds like standard advice until you are faced with a conversation you don't want to have. Don't give in to the impulse to hide in your office or avoid it. Have the conversation! Have the courage to say what is on your mind clearly and without emotion. This is about taking up space and speaking up. This does not happen enough, and it should.

I had a mentor early in my career who advised me never to lose sight of the fact that we all have an unconscious tendency to bring the dysfunctions of our families to work. He talked about how this can lead to expressing ourselves in less-than-ideal ways and to ignoring what he called the "moose on the table." We take things personally, inappropriately applying unrelated feelings about past hurts and frustrations to new challenges and even assigning blame where it does not belong. That insight has stayed with me, and now I, too, use the expression "moose on the table" as an icebreaker before addressing something unpleasant. It's become such a habit that colleagues also started using the expression, which makes me happy. They say, "I am putting the moose on the table," when they are ready to have a difficult conversation. It takes some air out of the balloon and makes it easier to start a dialog.

Have the conversation! Have the courage to say what is on your mind clearly and without emotion.

A SUCCESSFUL "DIFFICULT CONVERSATION" BEGINS WITH LISTENING

I learned long ago that one side of the story is never enough. Voicing your opinion is not worth much if you do not know what you are talking about, and the only way you can acquire knowledge is by listening. There are leaders who do not want to hear anything negative.

When I was in a management role in public accounting in the early 1980s, around the time when records were first widely computerized, I learned the hard way that productive but difficult conversations begin with listening. There was a mandate for all data to be automated by a certain date. I visited one of our branch offices after the deadline, expecting the paper documents to be digitized. When I was handed actual paperwork at the beginning of the meeting, I realized that little toward that goal had been met. I was not happy. I remember crumpling up the paper into a ball and throwing it on the table as I said, "You need to get this on the computer." I packed up my stuff and left. Thinking about how I behaved makes me cringe. I would not do that today.

At the time I believed I had to present a tough veneer in order to be respected—although what I did was nothing of the sort. It was emotional, childish, and unprofessional. This behavior endeared no one in this office to me. The respect I earned was grudging. There was no need for me to be so dramatic, but at the time, I just did not know how to make myself heard in a more constructive way. It was the first time I was managing people who were tasked with changing how we did things, and I let my frustration show in a way that was unproductive. Instead of asking what challenges the office may have been experiencing in getting the information computerized, I walked out without giving the team a chance to speak. The embodiment of how *not* to have a difficult conversation.

We drive people away when we do not know how to express our frustrations without getting angry. We drive them away when we do not listen. Eventually, the office did make the change to computerized filing, but I did not create any allies in the process, and I had to repair many relationships I damaged that day—and it took time. I may have gained a reputation for being tough, but it was earned in the wrong way. I made an impression—the wrong one: some people who witnessed it still talk about the time I threw a ball of paper on the conference room table and walked out. I was actually lucky. The next time I went to see the team, they poked fun at me for my behavior. In their own roundabout way and through laughter, they were giving me valuable feedback. I heard it loud and clear and never reacted that way again.

Today I handle similar situations quite differently, although I still expect that if we say we are going to do something by a certain date, we do it. Now, if that doesn't happen, I ask what went wrong and try to understand the issues that prevented completing a project on deadline. If there is a monumental set of deliverables, we try to break them down into smaller subsets of work, and we assess progress by setting manageable goals. I try to understand any underlying or systemic issue that prevents something from getting done and ask people to work on solutions. I still have high expectations, but I am an ally, not an adversary. I am a listener, not a know-it-all.

Productive but difficult conversations begin with listening.

Fairness and Transparency Should Guide Difficult Conversations: The Aetna Acquisition of Coventry Health Care

In 2014, when Aetna acquired Coventry Health Care, I was responsible for the integration of the two companies, an experience that helped prepare me for the integration work during and after the Aetna/CVS Health merger. One of my priorities in leading this work was to make sure I continuously communicated with our team members about the changes we were making and how they would be affected by those changes. There would be so many exciting developments to discuss, but there would also be the inevitable pain points—it's human nature to welcome some change but not all.

Once the merger happened, we had two people for nearly every job, so-called redundancies in human resource parlance. Each person had to be evaluated on his or her individual merit. If we did it right, everyone from each company had a 50-50 chance of keeping their job—and the same chance of losing it.

It is not an easy task to merge the teams of two large companies because you know some people will lose their jobs. I had a small team of people from each company to help with assessments. We met daily and used a process we had in place, adjusting it as needed. We had to make sure people who would be let go were treated fairly, particularly in terms of receiving assistance in finding suitable employment. Those who stayed would have changes to their responsibilities and expectations, and we had to make those responsibilities clear.

I held town hall meetings at every major Coventry site. I personally connected with 10,000 of the 14,000 Coventry team members, welcoming them to Aetna and establishing the honesty and trust we needed to achieve our broader goal of building a better company to serve our customers. Having that open, frank, and honest dialogue with colleagues made it easier for them to embrace change and therefore helped them remain focused on delivering great service to our members. I had a good partner from Coventry who ended up being my CFO.

We had no operational hiccups, so it was a successful integration. One of the board members said to me, "There's got to be something wrong." Maybe there were some little things we could have done better, but nothing relative to the big picture. I credit the phenomenal team who rose to the occasion and perfected the art of putting the moose on the table. Sometimes you cannot be transparent, but explaining the process openly and treating people with dignity mitigates the impact of difficult decisions during difficult times. The team did a great deal of planning and listening. We had frank dialogue, and we got to the best answers through inclusive listening.

Authenticity

One of the communication challenges companies have is establishing the trust required for team members to feel comfortable enough to talk about problems or difficulties they might have without fear of reprisal. Trust is hard to earn and easy to lose. Building trust within corporate culture begins with leaders who listen and show that they have faith in their teams.

Building trust within corporate culture begins with leaders showing trust in the company's team members.

THE BIGGEST MOOSE IN THE ROOM

Some subjects are taboo, and they should not be. The corporate world may be cutting-edge in many techno-logical ways, but it lags behind in other important areas. One of those areas is mental health. It is a crucial topic for society and vitally important for the workplace—but no one wants to address it. Because of my mother and upbringing, I have prioritized tackling mental health in the workplace, where team members experiencing these issues remain stigmatized. I try to be supportive of and helpful to people in crisis.

Sadly, this is not universally the case with many companies, where team members still feel obliged to tell their manager they are taking a two-week vacation when they are really checking into a mental health facil-ity. There are new mothers who extend their maternity leave by explaining they need more time with the baby when in fact they are struggling with postpartum depres-sion. Constantly feeling as if you must hide your true feelings puts pressure on us all, and it certainly affects team efficiency and the quality of their work. Pretending everything is OK creates a lot of pressure that eventually grows to an unendurable point. Then everything comes crashing down. You do not want to get to that point with a teammate. You want them to feel comfortable bringing their full selves to the job and talking about it. If you can get them help, even better.

The first time I talked publicly about my family's men-tal health issues, my mother's illness and suicide, was at a company town hall. Reflecting on that large meeting,

I realize that I did not go into it explicitly intending to share my personal story. At some point, I knew I would have to talk publicly about my past, particularly my childhood because it has profoundly influenced who I am, but I certainly had not planned to do it on that particular day. The purpose of the meeting was to discuss policy changes regarding mental health insurance coverage by emphasizing the importance of expanding access to both mental and physical health services. It was part of a broader strategy to recognize that overall good health requires seeing physical health and mental health as two sides of the same coin.

In the course of giving my planned talk about why it is crucial to remove the stigma around mental health issues—because it makes seeking help less stressful for those who need it—I told my story. It was a very organic moment. Standing there in front of so many people who were counting on me for their livelihoods and on whom I was relying to fulfill this mission, I had to. How could I not be honest if I was truly committed to being transparent, authentic, and honest? Qualities I espoused to my team on an almost-daily basis. It was difficult and emotional, but at the moment, it also seemed natural and appropriate to bring my past out of the shadows. I kept it simple but honest. That day, I put my beliefs into action. Telling my story helped create an environment where team members could be comfortable and not feel judged by talking about something that affected many of their lives and their families and colleagues. I believe it is critical for leaders to model the behavior they expect to see in others.

After that town hall meeting, many colleagues who had attended emailed me to share their stories and to tell me how hearing my story made it easier for them to talk about their issues openly. One woman wrote to tell me that her son had died by suicide, something she had never spoken of outside of her family. She explained that the town hall had been a watershed moment for her. She felt like she did not have to hide the tragedy of her son's death anymore. Hearing me talk about my mother gave her permission to be open about the sadness in her own life. It was a relief.

If we are going to be effective in addressing the most difficult issues in the communities we serve, we have to be candid about them. Straightforwardness destigmatizes conversations and helps establish healthier environments in which to do business. It is especially important coming on the heels of a pandemic and shutdown, which isolated people and led to mental health challenges for too many, including substance abuse, depression, and anxiety.[1]

I am fortunate to be in a position to make a difference in the access to quality mental health services. For me, it is not just a responsibility but an obligation. As a result, CVS Health has several initiatives across the company that provide grassroots support to colleagues, clients, and communities, including retail health clinics that provide screening and diagnosis of depression.

Even if you are not in a position right now to initiate or facilitate big systemic changes, you can engage by participating in projects that mean something to you. While the examples I just offered are specific to healthcare and reflect our power in the marketplace to create programs for change, I believe people with a leadership mindset can and should think strategically in the same way to create value in their own communities, businesses, and lives. Everyone can become part of innovation and change. Become part of a team that works on change or initiate it where you are. Get the help you need, support others on their journey, talk candidly, and don't judge too quickly or on incomplete information. Listen and learn. Share your own story with the goal of seeing solutions.

THE TRUTH ABOUT MENTAL HEALTH

People bring outside challenges with them to work every day. Nearly 10 percent of adult Americans suffer some depression in a given year, part of the 26 percent who will suffer some type of mental illness in that year.[2] We all deal directly or indirectly with people affected by mental health challenges. Recently, I had a conversation with a CEO who invited me to speak at a corporate event. He confided in me about his son's mental health illness and how it affected him and his family. Depression and other emotional difficulties have a ripple effect beyond the suffering person and touch all their loved ones. What position you hold in the company is irrelevant to the personal issues people are dealing with. Everybody has a story. Are people who need help getting it? I don't think they are. I wish more people accessed and used the programs available to them.

I often use facts and data when talking about mental health. My husband, Kevin, is the CEO of the Quell Foundation. His documentary *Lift the Mask* is shown in colleges, universities, and corporations across the United States and has been helpful in not only raising awareness but making it acceptable to talk about this difficult subject. You don't need a million-dollar budget to create content around issues that are important to you. It can start with compelling and cost-effective social media posts, YouTube videos, or TikTok reels.

Suicide is the 12th leading cause of death in the United States.[3] It's the second killer of those aged 25 to 34.[4] One in 15 college students have made a suicide plan.[5]

- On average, there are 132 suicides per day.[6]
- One in 20 American adults has had serious thoughts of suicide.[7]
- Severe major depression increased in youth to 9.7 percent in 2021 (from 9.2 percent in 2020).[8]
- The most frequently diagnosed mental health conditions in 2021 were depression, anxiety, and bipolar affective disorder.[9]

What can *you* do in your company to support good mental health, wellness, and well-being? Is there anything beyond your personal compassion you can offer?

Sometimes it can be as simple as checking in with colleagues. Postpandemic, I've begun asking people, "How are you *really*?" In other words, I'm asking because I truly want to know how you're doing, so don't feel you have to respond with "I'm fine" as a social nicety. Tell me what's going on. Tell me if you could use some support. Let's be honest with each other. I'm happy to report that it inspired others to ask the same question in the same way.

We have a number of mental health programs and services included in the insurance benefits we offer. In this dynamic space with a growing need, we continue to look at new opportunities to support colleagues and customers with their mental health well-being. We offer all colleagues access to an employee assistance program (EAP) and teletherapy services. We also have onsite mental health resources and social workers at select retail health locations. You can advocate for programs like these within your organization, and if you have programs like these, please access them when you need them. There is help.

We scrupulously respect each individual's right to confidentiality, but also support a broader environment of openness about mental health. There is still a crippling stigma in much of corporate America. We work hard to maintain an openness in our company by making it clear that it is OK to talk about these issues without fear of detrimental consequences if you seek help. CVS Health may be a leader in its commitment to reducing stigma around mental health issues and helping colleagues find good resources to assist them, but there are hopeful signs that we are not alone. My former employer, EY, started its highly successful "r u ok?" program, which among other services includes peer mentoring.[10] Such transparency could not come to the workplace sooner. I wish that this kind of openness had been available to help my mother. It might not have saved her, but perhaps it could have reduced her suffering. So, yes, this is a very personal issue for me.

REMEMBER THIS:

► **Put the moose on the table.** Be willing to raise and address important and uncomfortable topics. Be the person in the room who articulates the challenging truth everyone is thinking but no one else has the courage to say.

► **Find the calm in the storm.** Difficult discussions do not require you to be rude or hurtful. On the contrary, uncomfortable conversations are easier to have when empathy and understanding underpin thorny subjects.

► **Listen, learn, speak, repeat.** Make sure you have all the data you need before raising an issue. Make your best effort to understand how others may feel emotionally and intellectually so that your point of view is informed.

► **Check in.** Make time to ask colleagues how they are doing in a way that signals you mean it and you don't want a pat answer. And don't forget to check in with yourself—ask yourself how you're feeling. If you or anyone you know needs help, reach out for it.

Voices Should Be Heard, Not Changed

Welcome others to express their talents in their own ways and in their full range.

One of the obstacles I faced when I was being considered for the presidency of Aetna was unexpected. There were no concerns about my work ethic or ability to deliver results, but *in 2014*—well into the twenty-first century!—a consultant brought in by Aetna told me that I did not fit the executive profile, meaning that despite meeting all of the qualifications for the job, I didn't look like a CEO. I had brought with me a career replete with tangible experiences and visible accomplishments, but apparently, this was not enough. He said I was too short, too blond, and my voice was not deep enough. Worse, I wore too much pink. In other words, *I* was the problem. He suggested, actually mandated, that I take voice lessons to help me sound more . . . masculine.

I was skeptical but decided to give it a try. After a few frustrating classes, I remember calling my husband, Kevin, using my new phony deep voice and telling him, "I can't do this." Kevin said what I knew he would, "Come home. You *don't* need the job if you can't be yourself, Jonesy." After thinking it over, I decided Kevin was right. I told the CEO, "I can't continue with these lessons. I'm not going to deepen my voice; it's not who I am. My voice is my voice. And I'm not going to dress any differently either."

"Your voice is fine," he said. "Who told you it wasn't?"

What a relief! I continued to honor my Aunt Millie's example of strength and perseverance and her most valuable advice—to be myself—and landed the job. And for the record, I still love to wear pink.

I have long understood that working in corporate America would not be easy—I am, after all, a woman, and therefore know all too well what it is like to be the odd one out in industries dominated by men. I also know that many if not most industries, including healthcare, offer limitless opportunities at all levels for people from all communities, including women. There is a reason more women are leading health services companies. It is women who predominantly make decisions for their families' health: 80 percent of healthcare decisions are made by women.[1] Such ceiling-shattering appointments were a long time coming, and even now, many women in all fields continue to experience the remnants of an earlier time.

One of the ways we earn a voice—not a deeper one, but certainly a more powerful one—is by letting others use theirs, a lesson that hit home for me when I was criticized for looking and sounding a certain way. Likewise, when you take up space at the table, make sure you are also making space for someone else. The two are related—when we are honest about who we are and allow and enable others to be *their* authentic selves, we're all happier and more effective.

Cultivating a group of talented people who bring varied experiences, knowledge, thoughts, and experiences to a common purpose, where differences can strengthen the alignment around the mission, should be the goal of any organization. The unique traits and points of view of team members are what make the work exciting and the solutions to meet them dynamic and effective.

Stay true to who you are and allow others the same courtesy—not only is it empowering, but your authenticity, uniqueness, and experiences are the most important things you bring to the table. Do it with intention until the practice of making space for others becomes a habit. Give others the same space. It seems so simple, but it comes with challenges because of preconceived and entrenched notions about how we should look and act when we are in certain roles. Yes, there are a set of standards around professional behavior, and they can be summed up with one word: respect.

This is a visceral issue for me. I have no argument with the idea that businesspeople should be professional in demeanor and appearance. I do not, however, believe that all executives must look, dress, sound, and, most important, think exactly alike. It is too stressful and exhausting to put up a front to please others or to live up to a stereotype or a perceived idea of what a leader should be. Being yourself means you can focus on getting the job done without worrying about your cover story.

The voice lesson experience led me to ask myself if I, too, used appearance as a shortcut when evaluating others. I can honestly say that no, I did not, and do not. Being nontraditional in my own appearance, I know all too well the problems of decisions based only on parts of an individual's whole. Just by being who we are, many of us challenge conventional ideas of who leaders or executives should be. This is the real problem in giving more people a voice and inviting their participation at every level of business: accepting the challenge of "the other" can be scary. We have to stop basing our ideas about what leadership and influence look like on old conventions. Let go of the notion that all talent looks and thinks in the same way because, in fact, there is a variety of human capital, a myriad of people who can align with your mission and what you are trying to accomplish with a company. Give them the freedom to express their alignment in their own way. Everyone in the workplace has a basic right to courtesy and collegial respect. I honestly think it is one of the most fundamental ways we can honor our differences. It really *is* that simple. Respect starts with each one of us.

> It is important to stay true to who you are and to allow others the same courtesy— not only is it empowering, but your authenticity, uniqueness, and experiences are the most important things you bring to the table.

TALENT IS EVERYWHERE

Pedigree does not equal potential. Great people come from everywhere. I had no special background or connections when I started my career, but I've accomplished so many of my goals by staying true to myself and bringing my experiences to every table I have sat at. One of the most significant problems in finding the best and most diversified talent is the tendency to be too narrow in our searches. Limiting hiring to certain kinds of degrees, colleges, or programs may not result in the kind of diverse team that will serve your needs. I'm not saying to avoid recruiting from prestigious institutions. What I am saying is that you have to look at your current recruitment strategy and think about how you can include other venues.

Talent is everywhere. Have the courage to look beyond traditional places and take risks on people, go with your gut. So many people took risks on me when I was not quite ready, and I think they would say it was worth it. Likewise, I have gone out on a limb for unique candidates, which has paid dividends. Great people come from many different places, and if you don't look for them, you won't find them. Similarly, don't wait for leaders to find you. Aim and reach high when applying for a job. Explain what you can do based on your specific experience, even if it's unconventional. Learn how to express your strengths and assets in terms of how they can serve the company. It's a good way to show off your creativity and strategic thinking.

Recruiting habits can be hard to break. Many large companies hire most of their team members from a small circle of schools. The employment website Indeed did a survey[2] of hiring managers and found that 29 percent preferred to hire *only* from elite universities, while 48 percent said the quality of the institution played a "somewhat important role." Just 4 percent said they didn't care where a prospective team member went to school. In the same survey, 43 percent of C-level executives agreed that "top performers generally come from highly reputable/top institutions."[3]

One of the problems with this hiring strategy is a limited pool: The top universities enroll fewer than 60,000 undergraduates, just 0.3 percent of all enrolled students. The top 50 colleges enroll about 600,000, or just 3 percent of the student population.[4] That means companies can sometimes pay too much for a new graduate because we compete with other companies for a small group of people. It can also mean that far too many of those responsible for hiring settle for someone who might not be as good as another candidate simply because the first candidate graduated from one of the schools they focus on when recruiting. This results in a less diverse workforce. It also means missing out on incredible people who could make valuable contributions to your business and your industry.

Another radical idea hiring managers need to consider is ending the degree requirement. Yes, certain professions need special training like clinicians. Before the pandemic hit, several large companies announced that they would no longer require applicants for certain jobs to hold a four-year college degree. It's smart but an idea that isn't showing up enough in business practices. Hiring is still often done in terms of the degree someone has and where he or she is from.

Many companies, including CVS Health, require a bachelor's degree and sometimes a master's degree for certain clinical jobs. For many other roles, we don't require formal degrees. We're interested in experience and cultural compatibility. Experience can be acquired in many different ways. Someone who has initiated, organized, and implemented a community project successfully might have the right experience for many positions, even if they do not have a certain kind of college degree. We are open to people with unconventional backgrounds. We have to be.

Universities no longer have a corner on knowledge, skill development, or networks. The Internet, including online learning, has changed that. Some forward-thinking companies *are* waiving degree requirements for many jobs, and they are doubling down on in-house education and training to recruit and upskill promising talent. Some hiring managers are also working to focus on developing individual competencies, including specialized knowledge and strategic thinking skills.

The bottom line: when you are in a position to contribute to the hiring process, advocate for an expanded view and encourage taking risks on candidates from all kinds of learning and experience backgrounds. One of the places we actively recruit from is the military veteran community, which in itself is an extremely diverse group of people. US veterans are a large part of our consumer base and our workforce.

In addition, CVS Health has established a national colleague resource group called BRAVE, whose mission is to support veterans in our communities and to create a welcoming work environment for veterans. As a result, we've been recognized on the Military Friendly Employer list, provided to service members and their families each year to help them discover the best post-military career opportunities available.

Why do we do this? Because we recognize the value of military service and know that veterans' skills and experience are unparalleled. We have hired many top team members using this strategy. Over the next few years, millions of service members will transition out of the military. We want to recruit as many qualified veterans, current Guard and Reserve members, and military spouses as possible across all parts of our business. We also offer special training to managers to help those unfamiliar with the military to decipher military experience and equate it with corporate experience. The training is highly effective.

WHAT DO YOU LOOK FOR?

A vibrant and broadly representative work environment is important not only to reflect, know, and understand the communities we serve but to ensure we have cast a wide net to find the kind of talent and creativity that will keep the business thriving. It is so much more than putting together a group of people who merely look different but who might end up sharing similar educational backgrounds, life experiences, and cultural values and traditions. We use many approaches to build inclusive teams. Many are practical, such as recruiting from within by identifying team members who have demonstrated potential and nurturing that potential. Aside from experience and knowledge, those less easily quantifiable "qualifications"—enthusiasm, energy, curiosity—are often exhibited by team members who are eager to develop, learn, and exceed. Be that person—it's a great way to get noticed. Be a cheerleader for others who may have unconventional backgrounds and experiences. I am a cheerleader of people and I do it through support, coaching, and listening.

I have worked with one colleague for more than 20 years. When I first met her, we were both early in our careers. She didn't work for me, but our jobs intersected, so we were able to get to know each other. She had an accounting degree from a small college in Pennsylvania, which is known for being strong in that field. My colleague learned about the job from a friend who used a company referral program (still a great recruitment strategy!). It was evident from the work that she had intellectual curiosity and a passion for always being better than she was the day before. At the time, her job involved pulling together financials for her division. I was the finance controller for her leader, the head of corporate finance planning. She remembers that even back then, I was clear about expectations. "I knew when you were disappointed in my work," she told me, "but I appreciated the directness. I've worked for people who would have the same reaction whether I epically failed or succeeded, and that's not helpful."

I'll take that as a compliment because it reinforces one of the threads in this book. In order for people to be accountable, they have to know what is expected of them. We owe our colleagues honesty and clarity. One of the first times she prepared a report for the executive management team, she shared it with me for review and feedback. My response was along the lines of, "I can't believe you gave this to me," along with some pointers on what needed improvement. It was somewhat harsh feedback, but it actually helped her improve at creating executive management presentations. She is still with the company and has become an expert practitioner and a versatile executive who has coached and developed many talented people and knows how to self-advocate. The only thing I would change about that long-ago interaction is being more diplomatic in how I coached her.

Aside from experience and knowledge, those less easily quantifiable "qualifications"—enthusiasm, energy, curiosity—are often exhibited by team members who are eager to develop, learn, and exceed. Be that person—it's a great way to advance in your career.

While recruiting people with varied experiences is important, it is equally crucial to seek them out for yourself. That doesn't mean you have to change jobs or companies. You can help with a project at work, volunteer for a candidate you support, or perform acts of service in your community. This is something I learned from Aunt Millie: make yourself better by doing that which improves the lives of others. Companies care about those things. When I see someone who has the right work attitude and experience and demonstrates that they are passionate about their interests and their communities, that signals to me that the person is deeply engaged and outer-directed. They are a potentially strong candidate. I get excited about the potential in a person, and I want to see them fulfill it.

This is a lesson I saw, modeled, and learned from Aunt Millie, whom I watched volunteer for many local political campaigns and community organizations even while she was working full-time in the factory and raising us kids. She did piecework at Carter's, which meant she was paid based on how many garments she could finish in a day. When she came home, exhausted, she would cook us dinner and make sure all our needs were met. When she retired, she committed to getting a senior center built, which didn't exist in Ware at the time. She volunteered for Meals on Wheels, and she wrote grants that resulted in funding for transportation for seniors. She was successful at all of it. When I look for talent, I seek out the Aunt Millie's of the world. That's who I want to be and want to hire. People who are never too big for their britches (a favorite saying of Millie's) and who don't settle for anything less than the best they can do. I expect this of myself, and I look for it in others.

When we're recruiting, we want people who are not afraid to bring new ideas and ways of looking at problems. We work hard to ensure that everyone feels welcome to share their views throughout the process. When we advertise for jobs at every level, we focus on the ability to deliver on goals and use words like "proven track record," "demonstrable results," "collaborative," "partners with," and "assists others." These are not just empty words. Our job postings convey that we do not filter out candidates based on what you look like or how you identify or what college or university you attended if a degree is necessary for particular jobs like nursing or other clinical roles. As long as you can work as part of a team, produce results, and are open to points of view other than your own, we want to talk with you. Our interview process ensures we are interviewing candidates with a variety of experiences and a variety of people who do not all look the same or have the same life experiences so that from the very first encounter, a prospective colleague can see that the workplace is comprised of individuals from everywhere.

They encounter people who look like them and who think like them but also those who don't—but who still align around common goals and values.

A big area of focus is also to fill and expand the pipeline of talent to ensure we have qualified team members in the future. CVS Health offers programs designed to encourage students to think about STEM careers in the health services as well as job training programs for adults looking to change careers. We have workforce innovation training centers located in eight major urban areas.[5] These centers extend outreach and support to under resourced communities and to the disabled, a too often overlooked talent pool. We've also established partnerships to promote workforce innovation and training. Through a partnership with the National Consortium of State-Operated Comprehensive Rehabilitation Centers, we have opened mock pharmacies at rehabilitation centers around the country. Mock pharmacies provide opportunities for students who are training for roles as certified pharmacy technicians and retail sales associates to practice what they are learning in the classroom before entering the workforce.[6]

I'd like to think that Aunt Millie would be proud.

THE MOST IMPORTANT D WORD: DEVELOPMENT

Getting the best out of all team members—and yourself— requires consistent skill and career development. It's about identifying what people are good at and creating an environment that enables the sharpening and advancement of skills that suit the personality and style of the team member. That's what I mean by letting everyone sing in their range. It's also about expanding that range, pushing beyond it but respecting the fact that not everyone will do everything in the same way, yet still achieve amazing results.

Let people try new things and have a willingness to put *yourself* in unfamiliar situations. Advocate for those around you to take a chance and fly. One company I worked for early in my career had a strong and effective talent program. They were intentional about putting a management process in place that gave potential leaders a great deal of visibility. We gave management a scorecard to check to see how they were doing in terms of making sure high potential people were given a variety of opportunities to learn about different aspects of the company. We measured our success in part in terms of team-member mobility.

You also need to take risks on people. People have taken risks on me throughout my career. Maybe I did not know everything required for every job, but I was willing to try. This is one of the reasons I like the development model common in public accounting, which is essentially mentorship. As a young accountant, I worked with senior professionals on a variety of projects and businesses. This process exposed me to an assortment of challenges. I was in the thick of it. It is important to be facile in public accounting because you never know what kind of client will come your way. It could be a manufacturing company, a healthcare system, a retailer, a nonprofit, you name it. Working alongside more experienced team members gave me the benefit of learning on the job and the chance to develop my skills while I was using them. This mentor model gave me the opportunity to interact with the most senior-level people in the organization. These senior managers would give me real-time feedback, which I may not have thought of as development at the moment, although it clearly was.

As an accountant, I didn't specialize in insurance until later in my working life. Development was a key part of my growth at one company where I spent 18 years. That's where I learned about management. I was skeptical when it came time to do a human resources rotation, but it was a real "aha" moment for me. I was put in a position where I had to grow people, which meant giving them honest and useful feedback, which was sometimes difficult. It didn't feel good when I didn't do it the right way. The first couple of times I had to deliver constructive criticism to a colleague was uncomfortable, to say the least, and that colleague has confirmed that! I wasn't as polished or as effective as I became with practice and time. But that's part of the bargain you make with yourself (and your colleagues) when you commit to learning and expanding your skills and knowledge. You will make mistakes, but you have to do it anyway. Learn from them and do better next time. Apologize and move on.

I have always tried to view any job I had that involved managing people as part team member with individual professional obligations and goals and part coach. The best athletes have coaches. Likewise, the best managers should view coaching and feedback as part of their jobs. Look for coaching moments. Don't expect people to get better on their own. Yes, it's possible, but it's not preferable. If you wait for a semiannual review to give someone feedback, no one will remember it months or even just weeks later. If you look for coaching moments when they occur and act on them, it reinforces the lesson and it is more memorable because the person is learning while doing.

Not everyone is talented in every area, but you want to round yourself out as a leader and as a person to find out where your skills lie. Let's go back to my accounting colleague. Early in her career, she lacked self-confidence, as so many of us do. But I saw that she had good instincts, and she was smart, driven, and collaborative. She was afraid she might not be able to do the job, but she was also willing to learn and to be vulnerable. She took her accountability for delivering on promises and obligations seriously, even though there were times when self-doubt crept in. When she recognized she wasn't good at one thing but better at another, she was upfront about it and pivoted. It you don't try, you never really find out where your talents extend. You have to be willing to do things you are afraid of because you might be good at them.

> **I have always tried to view any job I had that involved managing people as part team member with individual professional obligations and goals and part coach.**

You can only do that if you are supported by your work environment and company culture, which I believe is sometimes the missing ingredient of corporate development. People do their best work when they feel supported personally and professionally. One of my former colleagues, whom I kept in touch with, was struggling at her job. I encouraged her to join me at my current company. "This was pivotal for me," she told me. "I was struggling at that time, commuting a long distance in and out of Philadelphia and working long hours. I was exhausted. I had little kids then and wasn't spending much time with them. I was not healthy. I needed to reclaim myself personally. When I said to Karen, 'I have to do something different,' she said, 'Come here,' asking me to join her company. 'You can work from home. You don't have to move to Connecticut.'"

You earn a voice by letting others use theirs. And when you take up space in a meeting, make sure you create space for someone else at the table.

This was around 2008, so working from home while being in management for a corporation was still radical. Now, of course, it has become much more commonplace. Actually, she had initially declined my offer because she had a difficult time believing it would work. I insisted. "You have my commitment," I assured her. Then she shared with me some health struggles she was having.

"It's going to involve recovery time," she told me, "so I need your support." "Whatever you need," was my answer. She had surgery in January 2011. It was successful, but there was a period of time when she was healing and had to focus on her recovery. It was all worth it because having good health is important; she is a valuable colleague and plays a critical role in the financial health of CVS Health. When you find good people, support them. And if you can, take them with you on your journey.

Development is also about team building and encouraging camaraderie. That's why I have always encouraged charity events involving leadership and other team members, as a way to build strong relationships and loyalty and to reinforce the importance of the community. We can learn about each other more fully and come to understand our different personal styles as strengths. It encourages people to sing in their range.

I remember one such community engagement that took place at a group home for children in Florida. These children were placed because of a court order, sometimes because they didn't have a parent or there was some turmoil in the home. We gave the children Christmas presents, brought Santa Claus, and even had a snow machine to make snow. Since the children's home was in Florida, some of the kids had never seen snow before—it was a first for many. Watching what unfolded when the kids opened their gifts was so interesting—and moving—for the team.

These are children who have nothing—limited clothing, no games, electronics, or other devices most other kids have. We bought computer tablets for each child we were visiting with. One boy opened his tablet, looked at it, and said to his friend, "Oh my goodness, Michael, this is what you wanted. I will give it to you." It moved most of us to tears. Michael had not yet opened his gift, so he and his generous friend didn't realize they had both received the same tablet. It taught us all something, not least, that often people who have the least seem to give the most. It was transformational because we all saw each other in a vulnerable moment, with our defenses down. This recognition of our common humanity is an essential part of diversity, tolerance, and understanding. Seeing each other's "soft spots" makes us better equipped to accept our differences. That is truly personal and professional development. This is an important part of being in the community. These moments matter in terms of building a culture of understanding.

Development Is Currency

As CEO, one of my first moves was to raise our minimum wage. Investing in employees by paying them adequate wages generally improves efficiency, and leads to better performance, higher customer satisfaction, and increased morale. Beyond addressing minimum wage, the pandemic led to a war for talent. To be truly competitive and attract and retain talent, you have to offer more than money. People know the value of opportunities that expand their skills and broaden their experience. We continue to manage the talent crisis by making our compensation more competitive and providing what our team members find valuable, including training opportunities, skill enhancement, work-life balance protocols, and better-quality work environments.

LET EVERYONE SING— AND LISTEN TO THE SONG

I had the opportunity to work with a distinguished cardiologist, academic, and public servant. The doctor was a member of two presidential administrations and has gone on to direct important public health initiatives at large corporations. When I met him, he had been hired to head the foundation of one of the companies I worked for. Although he was new to the corporate arena, the doctor brought a wealth of experience to the position. A brilliant physician, his passion was to impact public health. This was just one reason I was and remain a supporter. When we had meetings, there were times when people would walk into a room, and no one would say hello to him. Little things like failing to extend a greeting send huge messages. Whether it was thoughtless behavior (there are many self-absorbed people in and out of corporate life) or something more malign, I do not know.

Maybe it was because of his naturally gentle demeanor, but he was sometimes reticent to speak up in meetings when we needed his viewpoint and knowledge. "When I first started at the company, I had come directly from academia," he explained recently. "Karen encouraged me to have a strong voice and not back down. She made me think about the times when I say something to appease a particular audience so that its members would not be uncomfortable. Karen made me feel that there was always someone in the room looking out for me, which gave me a certain level of confidence going forward in the corporate environment." I am glad he feels this way, and I try to encourage a safe space for speaking up and out. I do not want anyone to feel alone in a crowd—or a meeting. I let him know that he didn't need permission to speak.

REMEMBER THIS:

▶ **Embrace the difference.** Look for people from diverse backgrounds, experiences, and perspectives, not just the ones to which you have grown accustomed. Reevaluate your recruitment strategies and think about where the people you need might be found and go there.

▶ **Go to the source.** Learn about customers where they live and see the world through their eyes. This practice makes you more educated about those you're serving, but it also works to open your mind and be more accepting of different people and ways of doing things.

▶ **Compassion is part of good business.** Being able to empathize with customers and colleagues develops your people skills. But it also gives you a greater perspective on solving pain points and understanding the needs of those you serve and those you work alongside.

▶ **Give everyone a shot at success, no matter who they are or what they look like.** Do your part to ensure all team members have opportunities for professional growth and development and that all colleagues are part of the fabric of a business.

5

The Path to Leadership Is Never Linear

Get out of your lane.
Say yes, even if it's not the job you want.

The most unexpected turn in my career trajectory came when the CFO of a national health insurance company, the late Jim Stewart, asked me to work in human resources (HR). At first, I was puzzled; as a finance person, the last place in an organization I thought I would be effective in would be HR. As I thought more about the opportunity, I had the biggest "aha!" moment of my career to that point: people are the most important asset of any organization. This seems patently obvious, but at the time I was so focused on finance that the importance of understanding people and their talents didn't occur to me. Suppose my ambition included someday leading a business or organization. How could I do that without understanding how to identify talented, capable colleagues, including how to motivate, inspire, and compensate them?

I accepted Jim's offer—and its challenge—and took what turned out to be an incredibly fruitful and educational part of my career journey. I gained an understanding of talent acquisition, management, and compensation packages and learned about the strategic movement of people into new areas for their own development. The opportunity to create new policies suitable for a workforce that took advantage of the talents of women and other underrepresented groups, such as joint job sharing and work-at-home policies, was not an idea that was widely discussed at that time. I received flack for even bringing it up. But I worked through the skepticism and created some of these programs.

It was only after I took the position in HR that I understood the job was crafted by Jim for a specific purpose: many finance people rotated in and out of the HR and other nonfinance departments so that the current leadership could see us perform in a variety of circumstances as a way of learning who had the right temperament and talent. It was also a way of helping future leaders learn all aspects of a business they might be running someday.

This experience taught me to take every job offer or opportunity at face value and not to discount it because it wasn't in my "lane." My acumen for accounting, problem-solving skills, good judgment, professionalism in representing the company, and leadership ability could have value in many different areas of the company—and gave me a chance to learn. Indeed, as I moved through my career, I realized that embracing my skill set and unique traits and applying them to different situations made me more effective and authentic as a leader.

The bottom line: Don't reject an opportunity out of hand because it does not look like it is on the straight path to where you want to go. Have the courage to try new things because you never know what impact they will have later in your career journey. You will learn things that will help you as you grow and evolve as a manager and businessperson. It's also possible that you will find a niche that you had not considered. That's why it's somewhat disappointing when a colleague turns down the chance to learn about another aspect of their business or company. I get it: It's scary to make a move into an arena that is completely new. It's uncomfortable. That discomfort can be positive, your driving force. Get out of your comfort zone. That's what leaders do. Many people start on one path and end up on another, and that's OK. I started out in public accounting and ended up in healthcare, my primary goal—even though accounting may not be the obvious way most people think of entering this field.

Every day, I would commit to doing my HR job enthusiastically, asking questions when necessary, absorbing the answers, applying them to new issues, and bringing as much value as possible to all my interactions. I did my best to deliver results based on expectations. That's what I look for in others—what did they do to meet goals? If they fell short, how did they handle it? Leaders don't bat a thousand every time. I look for people who handle pressure, new situations, and challenges outside of their expertise with grace, curiosity, and determination.

It was the case for me—at one time, I was not described as someone strategic (no one would say that today). That was an aspect of my work that I had to grow into, and it took practice. This was true when working in HR and other managerial roles. The common thread of my successes was my focus on the job, meeting its goals, and gaining more confidence to take on the next challenge. The fact that I could talk about my successes was valuable when asked about the next job or position. Honestly, I never volunteered the information, and I think people should be less reticent about advertising their accomplishments than I have been.

If people asked me about goals, usually under the guise of being considered for another role, I would respond, but I have never been one to offer up unsolicited achievements. Over my career, the achievements and successes added up. The integration of two health insurance carriers, Coventry and Aetna, was a big deal, something I had not done on that scale before, but I took it on and demonstrated an ability to navigate the company through a difficult task. At that point in my career, the results spoke for themselves. I had been tasked with the job, and it had gone well. The outcome was visible.

Some people have no problem touting career achievements, but some of us don't promote ourselves enough. At the very least, there should be no shame in vocalizing demonstrable wins at work or in life—especially when asked, but even if we aren't. The problem is, you may not be asked, so you need to find the courage to say, "Hey, I did this," when it's relevant to do so. Timing is everything; if the opportunity to talk about your accomplishments arises, take it. Attaching it to learnings you can share is one of the best ways—talk about what you've done well in the context of what you learned from it.

LEAD FROM WHERE YOU ARE

My Aunt Millie deserves credit not just for my work ethic but for helping me think of myself as someone with something important to offer. I always wanted to succeed—for her, my mother, and myself. After Aunt Millie became ill, I started working at a national health insurance company, a job I landed because of my financial background and experience working with healthcare-related accounts at EY. I stayed with the company for 18 years, and during that time, I learned other aspects of the insurance business besides accounting. The company was interested in developing talented colleagues by allowing them to learn various aspects of the business. I was chosen for professional development because I brought a leadership mindset to the job. For instance, I did a stint as an underwriter, which I had not wanted to do, but it taught me a great deal about the insurance business I would not have otherwise learned.

I would not have used the word "leader" to describe myself when EY recruited me for my first job, but I acted from that place, thanks to lessons I learned in childhood. I had an inner drive to be good at what I was doing, which gave me the courage to take risks. Leaders must accept that they *will* take risks, producing other leadership behaviors and habits of mind.

Aspiring leaders develop a habit of mind that enables them to act from a place that assumes they are getting the next big job and operate from that standpoint, no matter how many years away the goal may be. They do this by consciously thinking about how a decision will affect both the immediate situation and the future by considering various possible outcomes. Not only does this mindset help you to develop the right skills, but it also increases your chances to have an impact because those in a position to consider your next big step will recognize you as someone who embodies the strength and forbearance necessary to run things well and manage people effectively. The key is to figure out what other traits are necessary for a leader at your company—and in life. On the other hand, you don't want to allow future ambitions to distract you from excellence in what you are doing today. Focus on all the leadership opportunities in your present job.

The good news about being a leader, and a transformational one, is that you can start modeling that person immediately. You need not be anointed: exemplify leadership no matter where you sit. You *will* make a positive difference by doing so, and you will be noticed. But first, you must face the truth about your capabilities. Own them. Do not—as so many of us who may feel marginalized, overlooked, or underestimated do—fall victim to your self-doubts. Everyone has them. Impostor syndrome can be a huge issue for anyone who has achieved even a modicum of success. Don't let it stop you; set aside your fears, put them in a box if you have to.

Here's what I do: I compartmentalize these thoughts in a box in my head. Next, I focus on the positive, what is going well, and where I can make a difference and show my skills. I also seek help when appropriate, if I don't feel confident about all the aspects of a job. I'm never beyond asking for advice and assistance. When I was tapped to do underwriting, which I knew nothing about, I told my manager just that. He said, "Don't worry, we don't need an expert in underwriting; we need a leader." He explained that we have many underwriting experts that need to be led. He said that he needed me to lead the group out of a challenging pricing strategy cycle, and I needed to turn it around. I called an underwriting pro I knew who had retired and asked him to come and work with me during my transition to take over the department. He became a member of my personal board. We would do town halls together, and he was by my side, even though he never spoke at these meetings—his presence was an endorsement and gave others a sense of confidence in me. And I did manage to turn the department around. Asking for help is a sign of strength, not weakness.

Once you identify an inspirational leader, and I dare say a transformational one, you can start modeling your behavior after that leader immediately.

Don't just volunteer for initiatives that interest you, especially those that might be visible to people in a position to notice your work, but also say yes when opportunities are presented to you, even if you think they may not fit with your perceived career trajectory. In doing so, you will learn more about how your industry works and will give others a view of your skills and what you can do. It does not have to be a new job, although in my case, it was. It could be project-based, such as organizing a conference, researching a business idea, and then writing and presenting a report.

STAY THE COURSE
DESPITE SELF-DOUBT

Am I smart enough? Am I good enough? Did they make a mistake when they hired me or handed me that new assignment? Wherever you are in your career, you have asked yourself those questions. Relax. We all have. The solution to self-doubt is to quell the voice of the angst-ridden teenager that resides within by asking yourself why you are questioning abilities you know you have all of a sudden. If the answer is "because I don't know what's expected of me" or "I am not sure my skills are the right ones to get this job done," then find out. If the source of your self-doubt is lack of clarity, ask for feedback. I suggest asking those who have influence or decision-making power over hiring (your boss, their boss, the human resources manager) where they think you can make the most valuable contribution.

Listen to what others think about your talents—they may see something you don't. Or if you are unclear why you have been asked to take on a new assignment, ask specifically how you will fit into the new role.[1] Better to clarify from the start than to wear yourself out with what will turn out to be—I guarantee you—baseless self-doubts. No one ever lost a promotion or an opportunity by asking a thoughtful question. When you ask a question, it's a way of saying, "I care about the job I do." That speaks volumes to those around you.

I have often been the rare female in an alpha-male environment. There are many more women in the room now than there were when I started in business, which is a great thing. I never allow the perception of being an underdog to provoke in me a feeling of self-doubt. One of the things that I do effectively is acquire knowledge. Knowledge breeds confidence. My thirst for information and data helps me prepare for high-pressure meetings, reports, and strategy discussions. If someone says something outlandish to me, because I have done my homework, I can (and I do) call them on it.

We've all seen it. Some people come into a meeting with a great sense of confidence even if they don't have the data, and that attitude alone can intimidate people. It can be an effective strategy—but I don't think it's a long-term solution. Better to know your stuff and learn what you don't know. Early on, I saw some people pull ridiculous ideas or "data" out of their hats just to have something to say, and they said it with such conviction and confidence that naturally it had to be true. If it is, that's great. But if, as is so often the case, what they are saying was not true, it was smart to be prepared with data that shows otherwise. Don't hesitate to do this, if you've got the goods. We all should realize that sometimes people say things with confidence to mask ignorance or insecurity. If you do your homework and you know *your* stuff, you are going to be able to challenge bad ideas or misinformation. That is what leaders do, no matter where they sit.

ACCOUNTABILITY

The best leaders with the most influence walk the path of trustworthiness. Trust is potent. Trust is power. I am always upfront with colleagues about what I know and what I do not know, especially during times of uncertainty, crisis, or change. I am a big believer in holding town halls. Even during times when you cannot meet in person (and in person is always best), like a pandemic, pick up the phone or have a virtual meeting so you can have a personal encounter. It wasn't only the social and cultural aspects of office life that we missed. We also missed those special moments of creativity and collegiality that only happen when people are together in the same room and somebody says something unique that you hadn't thought of before. That's because we all feed off each other's ideas organically, something that is not easy to do in a virtual meeting. You might have a chance encounter with someone in the hallway and stop to have a chat, and during this brief exchange, you could shift perspective. That's happened to me many times. Running into people on the way to someone else's office or to

Undated picture of Karen's mom, Irene.

Undated picture of Aunt Millie.

Karen and Kaymus (2015)

Becker College Commencement Speech and Karen receiving
honorary Doctor of Humane Letters (2015)

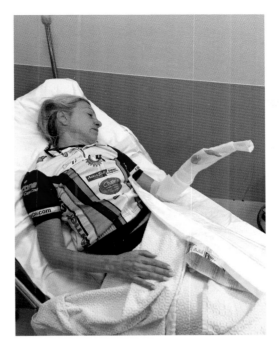

Cycling accident in the Netherlands (2018)

Karen informing Aetna Leadership team that
CVS Health will be acquiring Aetna (2018)

Karen signing Aetna stock over to CVS Health (2018)

Ware, Massachusetts Four-plex where Karen grew up. (2019)

Karen reading to a Ware Middle School classroom (2020)

Karen being informed by the Chairman of the CVS Health
Board of Directors that she will be the next CEO of CVS Health.

First day as CEO of CVS Health during the
COVID-19 pandemic (February 1, 2021)

Karen's first day as CEO of CVS Health (2021)

Karen and her grandson Michael, having cupcakes at the end of Karen's first day as CEO of CVS Health (2021)

Karen horseback riding in Montana (2021)

Karen and Kevin at the 46th Kennedy Center Honors (2023)

grab lunch can make all the difference. When you have the opportunity to work with people in person, don't take it for granted. Use the privilege to establish connections, develop deeper working relationships, keep communication open, and make accessibility paramount.

Make a conscious effort to be someone who is easy to talk to. Such accessibility and transparency in a leader are essential to setting the example of accountability that then becomes a universally recognized and shared corporate value. A leader holds herself to at least the same accountability standards that she holds everyone else to, and ideally to an even higher standard. She also expects colleagues to deliver on their commitments, and there is great accountability in that.

> **Use the privilege of working in person to establish connections, develop deeper working relationships, keep communication open, and make accessibility paramount.**

I try to give people latitude to be creative around solutions, but that freedom comes with clear expectations, and I expect my team to fulfill those expectations. You do not get a pass if you do not deliver results. Honor your commitments. People look for leaders who follow through on their promises and obligations. Of course, the reality is that there are a number of things you can control and deliver on, and there are others that are outside of your control. Many times you are working and leading in what I call "the gray." When working in unpredictable circumstances, nothing is ever black or white. There is nuance to accountability. Don't be flustered by the unknown; always work toward dynamic problem-solving and take full responsibility for the results. If someone acts on an unknown, makes their best effort, and owns the results, there's not much more you can ask for.

Such a high level of accountability requires a leader to be smart about the resources she has to get the job done, and no resource is more important than people. A good leader thinks of colleagues as a precious resource, treating them with respect, including how they talk to and about them. A good leader acknowledges the role others have in her successes, giving credit where credit is due. I have found that people are more likely to be accountable when they know they are treated fairly. A teammate who feels respected and whose accomplishments are acknowledged works hard to be accountable and, when challenged by a task, is more likely to be straightforward about what went wrong.

A leader holds herself to at least the same accountability standards that she holds everyone else to—and often to an even higher standard.

What you do and say as a leader has such a huge impact because people are counting on you. Don't squander that power by letting your emotions get the better of you, and losing the ability to be heard because people are not comfortable with you. That can lead to a loss of currency and relevance as a leader. It's important not to undermine your team's sense of accountability for achieving the goals of a specific project and accountability to you. In each moment, you want to be the kind of leader who inspires loyalty and trust.

The lessons I have learned as a leader in challenging situations have been enduring and have enhanced my leadership. A good leader does not assign a project, walk away, and not check back in until its completion deadline. There is a big difference between micromanaging and periodically asking how things are going, offering advice, and soliciting and listening to suggestions about how the task might be better accomplished. Seemingly informal, such a system of giving and getting feedback enhances accountability because it makes team members feel valued and thereby deepens their desire to succeed. At the same time, it engenders trust and willingness to be open about mistakes and misjudgments. It also allows for course corrections, if needed, before things go too far off track. A good leader is more than a decision maker. She is also a resource for her team. If you aspire to leadership, remember this: the more you are able to help the people you work with, the more responsibility and development opportunities you will receive in return.

In every workplace, accountability and transparency are intertwined, one reinforcing the other. With transparency, the leader's accountability is there for all to see. This is modeling desired behavior in its purest form. When team members understand why decisions are made, and how they align with and support the business's mission, they also see that they are part of the bigger picture. Their duty of accountability *matters* in a larger sense.[2]

REMEMBER THIS:

▶ **Ask for help; it's a sign of strength, not weakness.** Recruit advisers or those who can supply the knowledge or experience you lack so that your progress at work goes in the right direction.

▶ **Look for ways to show leadership.** Look for every opportunity to demonstrate your leadership potential at work and in your personal life. Take the job, even if it is one that does not lead directly to your goal. You are not sidetracked; you are showing your flexibility and mental agility.

▶ **Practice accountability.** I believe accountability is a muscle, and if you exercise it by doing what you say you will do, it eventually becomes second nature.

6

The Power of Learning by Doing

Continually seek out experiences, ideas, and opinions to broaden your view and develop insight.

---

remember my first scuba diving lesson: I was petrified. It wasn't all that long ago, so my memory of the fear is still palpable. Kevin and I took the classes in preparation for a vacation to a place known for great diving. Neither of us wanted to miss out on that experience. We started out in a swimming pool, and eventually, we'd venture into the ocean. I was OK in the pool, a controlled and finite environment. It was a different story when it came time to dive into the ocean. I remember thinking, "How can I possibly use a heavy oxygen tank to go underwater to look at fish?" I put my trust in myself, the instructor, and

Kevin, my "dive buddy," and I went under as I was taught to do in the swimming pool.

As soon as I was underwater, a huge sea turtle swam directly toward me. The average sea turtle is about three to four feet and weighs between 250 and 400 pounds. This one seemed bigger than that at the moment. My heart was racing, I felt as if my eyes popped out of my head, and I felt frozen.

The instructor, pro that he was, quickly swam in front of me, diverting the turtle's attention. While I was thinking, "This turtle is big. What do I do?" I also felt a certain amount of fascination. This scuba experience allowed me to get up close and personal with a sea creature in its natural habitat that I would not have seen if I had stayed on shore. It was one of the reasons we had taken lessons in the first place—so we could experience a world that would otherwise be inaccessible. It was new and fascinating, and I was not in charge.

I learned to let go of control a little bit that day; to be successful I also had to reinforce my ability to take things as they come and respond in real time and with grace. I may have wanted to freak out, but I didn't.

The other extraordinary aspect of scuba diving is that you can hear yourself breathing. Compelling and scary at the same time. It's an audible reminder of our humanity and that we are part of the ecosystem that makes up the Earth. When you go deep, it's deep. It helps you learn to focus on the moment and on your surroundings. That was a big opportunity for me to learn: trust, teamwork, and staying centered were magnified and enhanced skills during that experience. It brings me back to the advice Jim Stewart gave me earlier in my career: taking vacations feeds the soul and the spirit, but it also sharpens your job and people skills.

Likewise, during another period of time off, Kevin and I learned how to do a cattle drive on horses in Montana. Our group took cattle almost three miles to the top of a hill and down to their watering area. This was a good lesson for me in managing people in a professional setting, even though I want to be clear that I am *not* comparing people to cattle; I am comparing my own strategy of managing a large group. Cattle driving requires the leader to let the animals walk independently and make their way in their own style but within the parameters of where you want them to go. The interesting part about this is that you're not out front but behind them. You can also be effective on the side, giving them a wide berth but ensuring they are still within range. That's a leadership principle: Leaders don't have to be in the front. We can guide and lead from the side or even the back, allowing the team to progress.

I've also forced myself to learn how to play golf during my downtime because it is both a physical and a social activity that is still useful in business. I'm not great at it, but I can do it—and that's OK. Golf is a great way to enjoy time outdoors with colleagues, friends, and business associates. The first time I played in a group, I felt all eyes were on me. Everyone was watching. It was embarrassing but didn't stop me from swinging the club and playing the whole round. I held my own. That's a good lesson too. Even if you think you can't do it, try it anyway. Be a good sport. We often learn that lesson best when we're away from work. That's why, every once in a while, I will go out to play a round with Kevin. It keeps me in practice, and I enjoy some time with him in a beautiful setting.

We all know that time off is an important part of being effective as a leader. There are specific reasons why this is so—and why no one wins prizes for never taking time off from work. Time off is a chance to renew and restore, but it can also be a discreet learning time. Getting away from work and putting yourself somewhere your mind can wander gives us an opportunity to make connections that seem out of reach when we are acutely focused on a project. A deeper personal connection with ourselves is often the result of a vacation—and this can help us establish clearer goals, purpose, and intentions around work, our personal lives, and relationships. All of those make you more effective when you return to your desk. The improved physical health that comes from relaxing and movement and exploration results from destressing. Your emotional health also improves as time away from work provides rich ground for positivity, joy, and happiness.

These benefits lead to more innovative thinking. When we put ourselves in new environments and explore new places, we gain fresh perspectives. Novelty fuels innovation. Experiences that can seem unrelated to your job may actually help you connect new dots.

The other interesting phenomenon that occurs when you turn on vacation mode is that your team can become stronger. One sign of a great leader is when things don't fall apart when she goes away. Your time off is their opportunity to grow and learn without you. When your team has to solve problems without you, their competency increases, and their problem-solving skills sharpen. Their autonomy and confidence increase. As your team's ability expands, so does your capacity to work at a more strategic level.

Time off is especially important for people who find themselves working remotely, which has become more common postpandemic. Working from home has its perks but also has a downside: many of us may feel like we can't turn off the work. Vacations should be used for family and friend time and self-care. If you can't travel somewhere and change your environment, you can still try something you've never done. So many activities are within our reach: bike riding, gardening, hiking, singing, and dancing (my husband has caught me on our doorbell camera singing and dancing in the driveway after a run—I wanted to finish the song). Take a class, or indulge in hobbies that engage your hands and hearts.

> **Leaders don't have to be in the front. We can guide and lead from the side or even from the back to get our businesses where we want them to go.**

LISTEN AND LEARN

Probably the most significant learning that trying new things has given me is that my voice becomes more powerful and influential because I have learned to listen to and consider other people's knowledge, experience, ideas, and viewpoints before charting a new path. So while I make my own decisions, I only do so after first identifying what's missing in my knowledge or understanding and then seeking it out within or outside my organization. After all, the best experts often come from the most unexpected places. I would never have imagined gaining a leadership insight driving cattle in Montana, but I did.

I've added to my knowledge base and created space for original thinking by setting a clear direction with a timeline but not a rigid or defined route to get there. I sometimes free up the journey to solutions and decisions by reframing my question, which can result in new approaches and more useful answers. When it was first announced that I would become CEO of CVS Health, I created a challenge that invited team members to contribute their best ideas by asking colleagues a question I had asked myself. We crowdsourced ideas around "If you were CEO for a day, what would you do?" It was open to everyone in the company. That's where the company's new mission, purpose, and work behaviors came from. It's the foundation of our new minimum wage and scheduled lunchtime for CVS pharmacies every day at the same time. We also made positive changes to employee benefit plans.

Be curious about what's new, embrace changes that make sense for you and your business, and use your experiences with them to continue innovating.

MAKE IT EASY TO SEEK KNOWLEDGE

If you are serious about seeking new points of view, create a welcoming and encouraging place for everyone in an organization to share ideas without fear or ridicule. This approach is necessary to stay competitive, especially with the rapid advancement of technology. Team members at every level need to feel comfortable and secure enough to innovate and reinvent themselves and their jobs as their companies evolve. Once again, this comes back to culture.

Learning requires asking questions that not everyone is comfortable with, including the person asking and those on the receiving end. So you have to do it right if you are posing the question and be willing to lower your defenses if someone answers in ways you don't expect. I make sure that I preface Q-and-A discussions by letting people know I'm asking the question because I want to learn, not because I'm testing their integrity or accountability. I am sincerely interested in what they know or what they think about the work they are doing. I learned to put these conversations in context a while ago. When I first became an executive and team leader trying to learn as much as possible about the department I was running and the people I was assigned to manage—and motivate—my questions were sometimes taken negatively, as in "She's questioning our ability." Nothing could be further from the truth. When I am asking questions about accountability, I make that clear too.

I was at a pharmacy to learn about the process of filling prescriptions and verifying that the order was accurately completed. One of the things that the pharmacist and his team members mentioned was their customer service score, which was lower than they liked. They told me that they could improve their scores if they had a pill-counting machine. We provided the machine, and the next time we checked, the pharmacy service score was 100 percent satisfaction for customer service. That was powerful.

Some kinds of knowledge won't always come to you; you must go where the knowledge can be acquired. In the end, understanding what customers are feeling because they have told you directly (and you listened) and knowing from team members themselves what tools they need to do their jobs (and you responded) ensures better customer service and experience, as well as more dynamic and engaged colleagues.

More recently, I spent some time in one of our store pharmacies to observe the interactions between customers and pharmacists. This was on a Saturday, and the front of the store and the pharmacy area were busy. Given the volume of business that day, it was not the time to identify myself and further disrupt getting medicine into the hands of the people who needed it. I identified myself to the pharmacist and said I would be back at a quieter time. I also quickly asked the pharmacy technician about the long customer waits to pick up their medications. He replied that the new technology process being implemented was causing the delays. He was even more direct than that, saying, "Karen, it sucks."

When I returned to the store mid-week, I brought members of the cross-functional team responsible for developing and implementing new technologies in our CVS locations. The development team and I spent two hours with the pharmacists, and the technicians told us what was working and what was not with the new system. The conversation sparked my own questions and suggestions.

We covered much ground in those two hours. We learned valuable lessons we would not otherwise have known about in terms of improving new technology we had rolled out that provided virtual verification for every prescription filled. In the midst of the pandemic— or maybe because of the circumstances caused by the pandemic—I was able to identify and address an issue that had the potential to pose serious systemic challenges to our mission to provide the best, most accessible healthcare we could. We did not waste time blaming the pharmacy team or the technology development team on what wasn't working. Instead, everyone focused on solutions and making things right for our customers.

This approach takes leadership to a granular level but is not micromanaging. A leader needs to be informed. Sometimes, that means reading unfiltered customer emails, observing team members in their own work environments, rolling up your sleeves, and pitching in with frontline colleagues to identify and fix a problem.

In instances of learning, I do not ask questions to put someone on the defensive. I am curious about how they do their jobs, what the job entails, their challenges, and examples of their successes and frustrations. You can do all the reading you want about your industry and its trends—and that's an absolutely important part of learning—but nothing beats learning about the work firsthand from the people who do it daily. When a colleague recognizes that you are curious about what they do and you want to learn more about it, most are more than enthusiastic to share their knowledge.

The idea of recognition underpinned the Hero Award, which we give to people who go above and beyond. On the first day for a new colleague in one of our CVS pharmacies, one of our customers came into the store in distress. She was an elderly woman who suffered from Alzheimer's and didn't know where she was. She had been driving around the neighborhood not recognizing where she was and where to go. She finally recognized the CVS Pharmacy sign, and felt safe going into the store, even though it was not her local pharmacy. This new employee noticed that the woman seemed confused, so he approached her and was able to get information to call her daughter. He reached out to the daughter to let her know her mom was safe at the CVS store in the next town over, and she was able to pick her up and return her home safely. He had the empathy and patience to know what to do, a skill we prize. I learned of this situation because the woman's daughter sent me an email detailing the event and expressing gratitude. It's another way we can emphasize that our focus is on the health and wellbeing of our customers.

When I was engaged in a business integration (two companies merging), a big part of the merger's success, not just in terms of business but company culture, can be attributed to the time we spent early on asking questions about the similarities and differences in the values and philosophies of the two companies. To do this in an effective way, I created an integration team of people from all levels and areas of both companies that I thought could help build a new hybrid culture. No question was wrong, and no answer was dismissed out of hand. The first thing we did was spend time thinking about what kind of organization we wanted. We identified and defined this as a company that had an eye on the future, was inclusive, and valued innovation and accountability.

With that settled, we outlined our goals clearly so everyone on the team understood and could align around them. Second, we created opportunities for people from each company to work together in smaller groups to accomplish various combined goals. In retrospect, I think the early emphasis we put on learning about each other's ways of doing things and openly sharing the pros and cons of each without fear or judgment were edifying and helpful. I invested time listening to many colleagues to understand a corporate culture that was not familiar to me; I couldn't pretend I understood it or steamroll it with my own ideas. Our guiding principle enabled us to preserve the best of each company and seamlessly blend those ingredients into a recipe for a new cohesive team.

You can do all the reading you want about your industry and its trends—and that's an absolutely important part of learning—but nothing beats learning about the work firsthand from the people who do it daily.

A DAILY ROUTINE FOR LEARNING

Set yourself up for being learning-oriented with simple daily routines. For me, that means beginning the day with exercise and a quick look at the daily headlines and several cable news channels as I get ready in the morning. This routine helps me pull it all together and gives me a general idea of what's going on in the external environment outside of my company and business sector. Almost everything that happens in the world impacts the US healthcare industry; grasping current events helps frame my approach to the day's agenda and mission. I can connect the dots when I hear something at work or if I'm in a discussion with colleagues.

One hour of physical exercise, generally a run, weather permitting, or a session on my Peloton (I'm a fanatic!) boosts my thinking skills, and research shows I'm right about this.[1] During the day, I take time out to collect and organize my thoughts and do a mental check of how the day is going, including meetings and conversations I've had. This happens when I'm alone in my office, during a short walk outside, or in the hallways. Anything that takes me out of the moment, even for a short time so that I can reconnect with myself is helpful for unlocking creativity.

At night, I wrap up by reviewing everything I want to address the following day. As I run through the day's events, I jot down ideas. I look at my schedule and think about why a meeting occurs and what we want to accomplish during that time. This helps me keep meetings on track and efficient, and I encourage others who are holding their own meetings to do the same.

DO IT!

One weekend I was sitting at the kitchen counter doing some work when I got a call from the chairman of the board of CVS Health. It was that day I learned I would be named CEO. I'm also a huge Patriots fan, and I was wearing a T-shirt with the team's mantra emblazoned on it: "Do Your Job." My husband snapped a picture of me at that moment. I knew I was ready to take on the role of CEO. I knew it was my time. I was elated because I viewed it as an opportunity to transform CVS Health into a true consumer-focused healthcare company.

My enthusiasm for the job and my purpose in taking it is part of my overall philosophy: To do the next big thing . . . you have to do the next big thing. You're more ready than you might think you are. To a certain extent, you always have to learn to fly while you're in the cockpit of the plane, especially if you want to grow, learn, and expand your influence over things that matter to you.

While I have always had the experience to be 100 percent qualified to handle any job I accepted, I went into those jobs knowing there was much to learn because there will always be unknowns. You have to be willing to take those on. The truth is, while you may be wholly capable of succeeding at the next job, you may never be quite "ready" for the next big thing—but the challenge of learning new things is part of the excitement and experience of expanding your knowledge. This has certainly been the case for me throughout my career. You can't wait to be "ready" to do something new, or you will become stuck in your own uncertainty. Expanding your skills means taking risks. Growth and knowledge come from stretching into bigger and often unfamiliar assignments. I went from being in finance to HR to risk management. Then I took a role running a business in the dental division, and I thought, "Wow, I don't know anything about the dental business." But I knew I could learn what I needed to know and take up space to be heard and get the job done.

There's nothing wrong with feeling a bit anxious before you take a new job, especially one with greater responsibilities. If your eyes are open and you are willing to bring what you know to the role and learn what you don't know, there's nothing you can't do.

Learning is something that you need to keep doing throughout your career. The following are a few strategies to keep in mind.

Observe. I've learned what kind of leader and manager I wanted to be by observing how colleagues behaved in those roles and examining what styles are effective or lead to the most employee satisfaction and productivity. I vividly remember a manager in a company I worked in earlier in my career. He was calm and warm. He also happened to be one of the smartest financial minds around. The respect he showed people was obvious. As a coach and guide to those who worked for and with him, he developed many great people. This reflected well on him, and as a result, he had a powerful seat at the table and invited others to take up space at the table. This manager was effective in his job and a highly regarded leader—and that made a difference to the level of success he had, which was substantial. The people who worked with him wanted to do well because they admired him, and he made them know they were valued.

After he retired, another man took his place. His style was completely different. He worked everyone hard but never had a nice thing to say to any of them. It wasn't as if his predecessor didn't have high expectations for his team or set challenging goals for them to meet. On the contrary, he had very high standards, but he always showed gratitude and grace to his team, something the new guy never took time to do. I remember observing this style of management and understanding which man's style I would emulate—the former. I understand that the ego boost of getting a promotion can affect people's behavior—positively or negatively. Negative behavior sometimes works itself out over time, but in this case, it didn't. The manager did go on to do well in his career, but I am not convinced he did as well as he might have had he used a more inclusive and gracious management style.

I observed another executive who would pit team members against each other, believing the competitiveness would result in high-quality outcomes. I would go to work every day with a pit in my stomach. I was productive, but the work environment was not as pleasant as it might have been. I received a great deal of help from my personal advisors. I intentionally sought balance in life—by making time for friends, exercising, and just doing things I enjoyed during my downtime. Not everyone can overcome the feeling that they are going into battle every day in an effort to outdo their peers. I believe that teams accomplish more when they are not set up to be adversaries.

Sometimes, the most brilliant people have undesirable management styles like those I've described. It may work for them, but it's not who I want to be. We all have a choice, and I believe how you behave as a manager is a decision you have control over. The lesson is that you have to learn to lead in your own style. Just because your manager is a bully does not mean you have to be one. Take cues from others regarding what you think will work for you and what won't. However, I will say that my greatest learnings came from the harshest working environments because I clearly saw what I did not want to do or be as a leader. So think of those challenging experiences in the right way. Use both the good and the bad to formulate your own recipe for managing and leading.

Learn how to receive and offer constructive feedback. Like customer complaints, negative assessments from colleagues and bosses can be hard to hear—and often more difficult because a customer complaint is not directed at you specifically, whereas constructive feedback from team members is. Of course, hearing this feedback can cause you to be emotional. When someone says, "It's not personal," that's disingenuous because, of course, it's personal; it's about you. The best criticism is aimed at making you better. The greatest athletes need a coach because even the best of the best can improve their game. It's why I continue to use a personal board of directors, that close circle of trusted people who will be honest with me about what they think I am doing right, but also about areas of improvement.

It's easier said than done to say don't take it personally, but don't. If you receive constructive feedback from a peer, stay professional but don't feel obligated to change your approach if you don't think it will work. Listen and assess this information; decide if it makes sense to you. If it does, act on it. If it doesn't, talk to the person who offered the insights about it. Criticism is a gift, even though I know emotionally it's not an entirely welcome one. Instead, take the feedback and try it on. If it doesn't feel that it is part of your authentic self, you can discard it, but recognize that there may be consequences in doing so, especially if you are being asked to approach your job within the norms and culture of the company. Review what you're hearing objectively; there might be great nuggets of information that can help you improve.

Not all criticism is valid, but you do have to listen to all of it to learn how to discern what makes sense. I received valuable constructive feedback when I first jumped into that pool to learn scuba diving, and if I hadn't taken it I might not have been able to truly enjoy the experience when it came time for me to dive without an instructor.

I'm not talking about people yelling at you or telling you that you're doing something wrong without any feedback on how to do it right. That's bullying. If someone treats you like that, examine their motives.

At some point in your career, everyone faces an adversary that they may not understand. This happened to me during the process of being named president of Aetna. A high-level executive, I'll call "Peter," came to see me and said, "I don't want you to get this job. I don't like you." He saw the shocked expression on my face, but it didn't seem to faze him. "We're never going to be friends," he added.

"We will never go out to lunch or dinner together. Got it?" That's a tough thing to hear no matter who you are, or what position you're in. Bottom line: Peter didn't know me. Even so, he didn't think I was the right person for the job, and he was making it clear that I would not have his support. While I will never forget that encounter, I had to give myself the same advice I had given employees: he doesn't have to like me, but we both have an obligation to do our jobs well. I decided to take the high road and play the long game. That meant responding to him by saying that we both had jobs to do and a responsibility to work together to deliver for the good of the company. I continued to treat him with respect and never tried to undermine his work. Several years later, when I was named CEO, I received a very kind outreach from Peter who offered his congratulations and support in my new role. We reconnected and went on to have a collegial and productive professional relationship. By taking the high road, we had the opportunity to learn more about each other and we grew to respect each other personally and professionally.

Valid criticism and constructive feedback is different if phrased in the following ways: "You could have done this better by trying X," "Think about the way you're doing this," "Consider Y approach," and so on. We all have to be open to this information because we can all learn better ways of doing things.

Leaders also have to learn to offer constructive feedback. We're often taught to start with the positive and then move on to the criticism, but I think most see right through that approach. I like to be direct and say,

"I'm going to give you some coaching," and then offer my insight into what the colleague is doing less effectively and how they could do it better. I think this direct approach is more respectful of the person and their time. You never want to cause harm or have someone feel as if they are being attacked—it's not an attack; it's information that will make the team member more successful. The goal is for the recipient to absorb what they are hearing and give it consideration. I think you do that best when you use a direct, kind, and respectful approach.

> **If your eyes are open and you are willing to bring what you know to a role and learn what you don't know, there's nothing you can't do.**

LEARNING THE HARD WAY

To be honest, the risks you take when you seek new experiences don't always work out the way you expect, but that doesn't mean failure or unexpected consequences aren't opportunities for learning or innovation. You get better at pivoting and adapting when your adventures take a different turn, especially one for the worse. One of my travel adventures turned into a painful experience, but it resulted in meaningful innovations. You never know where, when, how, or why the lessons and learning will come, so always be open to them.

I got up close and personal with the ground during a devastating cycling accident in Amsterdam that severely injured my hip. It was only day three of a long-anticipated getaway. When riding a bike, you must learn how to clip in, improving the connection between your foot and the bike pedal. Three components help you: your cycling shoes, a cleat bolted to the bottom of each shoe, and your bike's pedals. The cleats engage with the bike pedals to create a secure attachment, which increases your cycling power and efficiency. You disengage by twisting your heel and releasing the cleat from the pedal. When you clip in, you're attached to the bicycle, so while you gain the power to ride securely, you also have some restrictions on movement. You give up a bit of control to be more precise and efficient.

I was riding on uneven cobblestone streets, and I was unfamiliar with that type of terrain or how I was supposed to ride on those streets. My riding buddy ahead of me hopped a curb, but I didn't see the curb in time, so I didn't clip out fast enough. Down I went with the bike! I flew over the handlebars, and my bike flipped on me. I fell on my left side, and broke my hip.

That experience didn't turn out to be the kind of reality-based observation I was looking for when I got on the bike, but it was eye-opening in unexpectedly useful ways. It was my first major personal healthcare experience, at age 55. Accessing and managing emergency care away from home, surgery, healing, and aftercare was nothing I expected it to be. It wasn't seamless and it was difficult coordinating all the post-surgery care that was needed to help my healing. What I thought I knew about European and American healthcare systems was challenged. Even while dealing with an acute injury and long-term repercussions, I noticed what was missing from my options and alternatives, both in Europe and at home—and there were a few surprises. CVS Health's Healing Better program was one of the outcomes of my accident in Amsterdam. Patients going in for any kind of surgery should know what to expect before, during, and after the procedure. I wanted anyone to be able to walk into a CVS and get everything they needed once they were home: a walker, a shower chair, and so on. Order it, and CVS will ship it to you before your surgery, so everything is in place waiting for you. This service brings vital products to consumers when they need them.

When you do go out on a limb and try something new, there is an exhilaration that comes, an energy that you can bring back to yourself, your colleagues, and your work. Never stop learning.

REMEMBER THIS:

▶ **Don't underestimate the power of grace.** Learning how to accept constructive assessments of our performance, work habits, and ideas is crucial in improving our performance. Not all criticism is helpful or necessary to follow, but some of it is, so we have to be open to all of it.

▶ **Set a destination and a timeline but not the route.** While it is important and necessary to have business goals, don't be too quick to dictate how to meet them. Leave the map open for exploration—sometimes, a detour can yield the best result. If we predetermine the direction, we may miss out on important insights gained from taking "the road less traveled."

▶ **Be open to questions.** Create spaces that welcome questions and exploration, where people can talk comfortably about what they don't know. Make a rule: no ridicule.

7

Leading with Empathy

The truth is often found on the other side.

Not long ago, I received an email from an elderly gentleman—I know that because he mentioned his age—who told me he was having difficulty scheduling an appointment for a vaccine. At the time, the CVS Health pharmacy was set up to accept appointments scheduled online only. The man explained that they weren't equipped to do that, and it was frustrating not to be able to call to make an appointment. The email included his information, so I gave him a call and introduced myself—there was a long pause on the other end of the phone. I admit to being amused at the silent disbelief of customers when I make a personal call; the joy of it never gets old for me. At any rate, I explained that I wanted to talk about what he had experienced.

The conversation provided important insight and learning for me. It made me think about what it was like for one of the most vulnerable communities to try and get the COVID vaccine. If one person found it difficult and spoke up, there must be many more who were not vocal about it. When we finished the call, I made good on my promise to the couple that I would see how we could work through the scheduling issue. We often tend to take many things for granted—in this case, the ease of scheduling appointments online. Turns out it's not easy for everyone. We did make a change and enabled customers to make easier walk-in visits without scheduling appointments.

When I think about leadership qualities, empathy is a concept that resonates because I saw it in action, observing my Aunt Millie walk through life as someone who didn't have a lot of material things to give—but one thing she had plenty of was empathy. It's not a soft skill or a meaningless trope. It's a skill that helps you see flaws in solutions and solutions in flaws. You access it by taking the time to think about an issue from the other side by putting yourself in another person's position. Doing so offers important lightbulb moments.

At one point in my career, one of our insurance members contacted me directly in a letter. She had a daughter with a diagnosed eating disorder, anorexia. In her letter, she explained that our company had denied a request to extend short-term in-patient services that she believed her daughter desperately needed to help her recover. It's not unusual for customers to write to the head of a company when they feel strongly about something, positive or negative, especially when it concerns the denial of coverage for medical services. I know I can't call every person who sends me a letter—but I read them all and take them to heart. This one hit me, however. It wasn't difficult for me to put myself in the girl's and her mom's shoes. Eating disorders are challenging to overcome without the right kind of support, and the consequences of leaving them untreated can be dire.

I contacted the mother to discuss her benefits coverage, review their access to resources, and express my concern for her daughter. I also checked with our team in the area that reviews requests from members about health services to see if they received all the information they needed to assess this decision. At the same time, the team requested updated information about the member's condition and the plan. The clinical team revised their findings and added more days to the in-patient treatment. We should never shy away from using empathy to question and reexamine our opinions and decisions when it's appropriate.

Once we approved the treatment plan, I called the daughter personally to tell her. She was excited, to say the least, especially since I made the call on a Saturday morning. "I can't believe you're calling me!" she cried. We had a nice chat, and I was reassured that this young woman would get the help she needed and wanted, knowing that so much success in treating eating disorders is a desire in the patient to get better. The following Christmas, her mother sent me a letter to tell me her daughter was doing well, thanks largely to the support she received during her in-patient days. Her daughter was also working with Feeding America and Teach for America.

The complaint from the young lady's mother also started an important chain of events. It resulted in changes in how we provide benefits coverage for eating disorders. We reassessed our policies and identified areas in our coverage that we hadn't considered that would be beneficial to members.

This experience crystallized there is a gap in consumers' awareness and understanding of the insurance benefits they have access to that help keep them healthy or get on the path to getting healthy. It is frustrating at times because I see the great things we do daily, but I wasn't clear on why the message wasn't being communicated well. Part of my responsibility is to learn how to do the best job of talking about what we're trying to accomplish. I recognize that we're not perfect, sometimes we're wrong, and we make mistakes, but we constantly strive to learn how to get it right for those who depend on us. Using empathy skills is a good way to do this. We shouldn't be afraid to appear weak—empathy makes us stronger. It can also give us an opportunity to tell stories about what we're doing to help people on their personal health journeys.

Another situation where I understood the power of empathy in leadership involved a young man, let's call him John, who had a rare form of muscular dystrophy, a difficult disease under any circumstances. John was considered for a complex surgery to save his life. At the time, this was a new procedure and it posed a potential risk to the patient's life; it was not a procedure that was covered by his health plan. John's complex health status factored into the assessment of whether this surgery was appropriate. We gathered all relevant decision makers around a table to review John's case and the data in relation to the procedure. Time was a factor.

The clinical team reviewed the medical information and ultimately the surgery was approved. Given the complexity of John's history, the clinical team had to compile all available data, including tracking down new information about recent outcomes from the surgery for other patients. The assessment indicated that the chances of the procedure succeeding—meaning extending John's life—were good.

Data is important—it comes from thousands of doctors and clinical experiences and outcomes. Decisions about procedures are based on science and data—but that does not mean that you should not consider the science from a human perspective. Data and empathy are not mutually exclusive.

Healthcare is a challenging environment. The care system is fragmented and the pace of change in medical advancements is accelerating. We are often working with customers during the most difficult times in their lives. We can make a difference by working to capture all relevant information and making a decision based on evidence-based clinical policies that keep the patient at the center.

John was still a teenager at the time and had undergone over 100 medical procedures. He was just one of Aetna's millions of members, a nonverbal quadriplegic with cerebral palsy, weighing just 55 pounds. In the process, something remarkable happened: I got to know John. Our inspirational friendship remained until John passed away in 2023.

EMPATHY MAKES TOUGH TALK EASIER

As I intimated at the beginning in this chapter, customers can be important gateways to empathy and learning about your business. You must find practical ways to listen and talk to them. This seems self-evident, but in my experience, for expediency and convenience, we can tend to regard customers as numbers and data points, not as individuals with valuable thoughts and experiences. Unfortunately, this attitude leads to many missed opportunities for the insight empathy offers. That's why I've reached out to individual customers throughout my career and encouraged others to do the same. In fact, I have long tried to take every appropriate opportunity to access customers and connect with them. Obviously, it is impossible to speak to every individual customer and client, but there are ways to keep in touch with those we serve.

We know sometimes some situations are really complicated and require a team who can handle a customer complaint that includes multiple issues that span several areas of the company. We have this with our Executive Complaints team, which takes on the most challenging issues that face our customers. Occasionally and when appropriate, I also pick up the phone for a one-on-one call with a customer who has issued a complaint. Of course, addressing every individual request is neither feasible nor reasonable. Still, complaints and criticisms can lead to fruitful discussions about policies and updating those policies when appropriate. While I would never override what a clinician says, a customer complaint will lead me to study all policies, clinical and otherwise, and understand whether they should be rethought or revised. Over the years, all the companies I have worked for have evolved their policies toward customers—and many of those changes came from empathy: understanding customer pain points and addressing them.

Admittedly, it's not always easy or comfortable to walk in someone's shoes. Often the invitation comes in the form of customer complaints. These missives—often sent in email forms on company websites, on social media platforms, and even in old-fashioned letters—are usually dealt with by customer service and never cross the desk of others in the company, which is unfortunate. A missed opportunity. Everyone in an organization should have access to common customer complaints and be aware of them since solutions to problems come from many sources. At one job, someone on my team told me that they could turn off all the customer complaints that come into my email and redirect them to customer service. Mailed letters could be intercepted, read, and addressed by other team members. I said, "Absolutely not. I want to see them." Complaints are useful indicators of how customers are experiencing your business, and they help you identify emerging problems, including systemic issues you might overlook or never see otherwise.

When it's appropriate, I respond directly. Some specific complaints do not require a direct response from me, so after I have read them, I send them to those who can help. If you decide to take this approach, I want you to be ready for personal attacks and even threats. People can be very emotional around bad experiences—especially in healthcare—and while it is understandable, it can also be upsetting. You have to put personal attacks in an emotional perspective, and of course, you need to take threats seriously, unfortunately.

A colleague of mine in another business told me about complaints he had seen about the cleanliness of his properties. It wasn't one or two over a year; it was many complaints voiced continually over several months. He didn't shrug off these messages. They prompted him to ask questions of his team about why the properties weren't maintained properly. He learned that his company had cut the budget for cleaning and maintenance, so naturally, diligence in keeping the properties neat and tidy had fallen short. He was not able to visit every single one of his business's locations, so the only way he knew about it was by reading customer complaints.

When someone takes the time to write to a company about something that bothers them, it's serious for them. We are all in a time crunch, so he respected the fact that people were bothered enough by the unkempt appearance of his businesses to go out of their way to tell him about it. He informed his team, "We're putting all that money back into cleaning and maintenance." Cutting corners or being frugal with maintenance didn't make economic sense.

This is a simple but important story because complaints that form discernable patterns indicate that you may have a problem that needs to be addressed. Of course, you can have one-off grievances: a disgruntled customer complaining about an isolated incident. But if you see consistency in customer frustration, that's an insight into what is happening that could be turning them off—and away.

As part of my long-standing mission to learn more and energize companies regarding innovation, I have always asked questions from the customer's and client's point of view. I try to put myself in their shoes, which is not hard because I am also a customer and client, like all of us, of many businesses and organizations. I look at products and services that people like or are popular—can we improve upon them and broaden access to them? I also look for gaps in services and products that I can help fill.

This shift in orientation generates a more productive and creative way of thinking. Obviously, we want products to be successful; otherwise, it would be foolish to bring them to market. But looking at the question of innovation through the customer's eyes helps us see relevant problems we may not encounter ourselves and then find the right solutions. Empowering colleagues to put the customer first changes the entire plotline. It gives team members a sense that their work has real meaning, that it's relevant.

It's important to be open to learning about new technologies that could improve the customer and colleague experiences. Embrace them if they work for the customer, and find ways to use them to increase employees' well-being and productivity. Be curious about what's new, implement changes that make sense for you and your business, and use your experiences with them to continue innovating.

Looking at the business through the customers' eyes led us to develop more personalized consultations with the pharmacist to build stronger, trust-based relationships, creating an incentive for the customer to seek out help from pharmacies and provide on-the-ground care, which lowers medical costs over time. The program gives pharmacists strategies to optimize medication use and helps them recommend appropriate vaccines, screenings, labs, and lifestyle changes. It also allows them to connect patients to resources, including care management and prescription home delivery.

A CVS pharmacist in New York used the program to support a member with a history of asthma. The pharmacist talked to the member about the potential benefits of a rescue inhaler. The patient allowed the pharmacist to contact her doctor to discuss whether a prescription was needed. When a customer comes in to talk to a pharmacist, they are usually in a situation where they need immediate care or service. By enabling authentic connections between pharmacists and patients at this point in care, we can help people when they need it the most, and we can create a relationship that makes it more likely for that person to seek the advice of a pharmacist before a health issue becomes more critical.

The program is now a critical part of our efforts at expanding effective preventative medicine, which lowers healthcare costs to both customers and the industry.

We have also elevated the profession of pharmacists and emphasized their importance in community medicine and health equity by creating a corporate role of chief pharmacy officer. Not only does this job help create a cohesive pharmacy strategy, but it also signals to our pharmacists that we take their role seriously—without them, we could not achieve our long-term goals of making healthcare accessible and community-based.

TAKE INITIATIVE TO UNDERSTAND ALL YOUR CUSTOMERS

Be proactive. Go where your people are. Learn what life is like from their perspective. I think of this as grassroots development. Go to the source.

One training session we created for senior leaders was to put them through a day in the life of a Medicaid member. Medicaid provides health coverage to millions of Americans, including low-income adults, children, pregnant women, elderly adults, and people with disabilities. Medicaid members generally are among the most vulnerable in our society, with limited resources to combat their socioeconomic and health challenges. It requires deep understanding and empathy to support where these members are coming from. We asked our senior leaders to address multiple situations that Medicaid members typically face. The first was to have our leaders fill a prescription within our system to understand this experience for individuals on Medicaid when they need to contact us to get prescription medicines.

In another simulation, a series of life events resulted in a customer having problems paying her bills and team members had to problem-solve. In the process, they came to understand that even one event that some may take for granted can devastate a person's financial situation. Other simulations provided glimpses of different circumstances or health conditions a person might have—a mental health issue or diabetes, for instance—to give leaders a broad sense of what our customers' lives can be like. Other simulations detailed how customers might not be able to pay their insurance premiums or how they could miss an appointment with their doctor because circumstances prevented them from following through. On a fundamental level, it opened our executive teams' eyes to what a person on Medicaid may experience.

I remember everyone who participated affirming that it was a learning experience. Clearly, all of us never quite understood what life as a Medicaid member is like. The understanding and empathy that came out of it had far-reaching effects. Our customer-facing team was more thoughtful when they interacted with Medicaid clients and asked more questions if someone missed an appointment. The reasons could very well have been a circumstance beyond their control. As a result of this team effort, the delivery of the service improved, and our customers were more engaged.

Improving efficiencies in Medicaid service delivery is important. This government program is a significant part of our overall health insurance business and the broader health system in this country. We need to do it right to meet the needs of our customers. Medicaid represents a large and important piece of the healthcare market. According to the Kaiser Family Foundation, one in five Americans use Medicaid.[1] If CVS Health is to administer even a piece of a program of that size, it must do it well, so it is pragmatic to try to understand the Medicaid customer.

While this experiential project resulted in new ways of thinking for Medicaid members to more easily access the services they desperately need, it also had a wider effect. Perhaps more importantly, it gave our senior leaders an eye-opening experience that developed their empathy skills, something they can apply to every aspect of their lives and careers.

As leaders, colleagues, and team members, we have to remember to listen. We need to give other people the space to share their insights. Diversity is built by welcoming all ideas and giving them a chance. You also develop yourself when you participate in developing others. You earn a voice by letting others use theirs. And when you take up space and use your voice, make sure you create space for others too.

REMEMBER THIS:

▶ **Empathy is not a soft skill or a meaningless trope.** Understanding how others feel or are shaped by your actions is a super-skill and a powerful way to strengthen your leadership ability.

▶ **Examine decisions from the perspective of the people affected by them.** This can be an intentional and very deliberate exercise. When thinking about the potential results of a decision, make sure you have accounted for all those impacted and how the decision will make life better or worse for them—consider all the potential possibilities. You may end up modifying that decision.

▶ **Learning from stakeholders is humbling and powerful.** Be willing to listen to the experiences of others; it's one of the best ways to flex your empathy muscle and make positive changes.

8

Responsible Transparency

Demonstrate responsibility through individual actions.

While I was chief accounting officer for one company's individual health insurance business, the decision was made that this business would be sold. This individual health insurance business provided benefit plans to individuals and their families. This challenging business requires a deep understanding of consumer needs and preferences. I was one of four people in the business's group who knew of the sale, partly because I was tasked, along with other team members, with putting the deal together. Such sales are not unusual for companies with multiple divisions when it makes sense. Strategies change, business needs evolve, and reimagining companies' structure, size, and scope can be part of those changes. In this situation, the work I was doing was discreet. I could not discuss the sale with the division's team members while the deal was being structured and finalized, including with its senior leaders. I respected and felt an obligation to comply with this directive. Discretion is important when selling part of a company, especially a public company. This is *always* the case. If rumors or innuendo flow into the marketplace, it can adversely impact company stock prices; it can also damage internal morale and productivity; clients and customers may be concerned with stability of services; and talented team members might leave.

After we had secured a buyer and the fine points of the sale had been hammered out, we announced the deal to the team. I did not lead the sale, but it was my responsibility to tell my team, and honestly, I was not prepared for the response I received. I gathered everyone involved into a conference room and told them of the sale in the most straightforward way possible. The financial team was upset for so many reasons. First, they felt blindsided; they weren't wrong that they had been in the dark about the sale. Second, they were now, in effect, part of the acquiring company, one that they were unfamiliar with. There were many unknowns, and they had many questions. Would they keep their jobs? Did they *want* to keep their jobs? Could they stay with the company they had been with, knew, and liked? Some were so angry that they were beet red and banging their fists on the table. People were in my face, yelling, "How could you do this to us? We had no idea! You've been asking us for information for weeks and months, and you knew the questions were all under the guise of selling the company, and you didn't tell us." They were right: I *had* asked them for information and could not tell them why. I was sworn to secrecy and had signed a nondisclosure or confidentiality agreement. I took that promise seriously. I couldn't even tell my husband. The team's reaction created an internal crisis. They felt betrayed. I understood their frustration. I realized how important consistent communication is in critical situations, especially those directly affecting people's lives and livelihoods.

I have never forgotten this episode. From then on, I vowed to use one of my accountability principles: tell people what I know and can share, what I don't know, and that I know things I cannot reveal. This doesn't make leading any easier, but it can help to establish a level of trust I had lost that day. If I could go back, given the confidentiality requirements I was bound by, there wouldn't have been more I could have told the team before the sale was negotiated. However, I would have delivered the news of the sale in a different way. I would have established from the beginning of my talk that we had their best interests at heart, and we did. I would have explained more clearly, with more detail, why the sale had to happen and what it would mean for their careers and roles going forward.

I told them we were working closely with the new ownership team to ensure everyone who wanted one would have a role at the new company. I knew that not everyone would be happy with the job or the new environment, but we did our best to ensure a smooth transition and that people would continue in the same roles where they had thrived in the previous company.

Once the sale was announced, we could be much more forthcoming with information, and I was as open as possible. We communicated consistently and regularly as we went through the next couple of months of integration. I told the team everything I knew and told them what I didn't know but was trying to find out. I answered every question they asked to the best of my ability. Once the organization moved to the new company, I went on to another assignment, but I never forgot the lessons of that sale.

It was absolutely a lesson on accountability and leadership. I was put in a position of working with 100 people who had to be kept in the dark until specific tasks around the sale were completed. Once the sale was announced, these people looked to me for information and guidance. It meant stepping up to the plate, being authentic, and understanding their concerns. I was young in my career, so I was learning as I was doing, and I didn't do everything right. It was scary and frustrating for everyone. I was able to repair some but not all of the relationships that were scarred the day I announced the sale of the company. Tinges of resentment remained in the air. Sometimes this is unavoidable because you cannot control other people's emotions, but you can mitigate negative feelings through accountability, transparency, and honesty.

STRIVE FOR ACCOUNTABILITY EVERY DAY

Everyone wants to feel good about the people and companies they work with and invest in. More than 70 percent of consumers say they want to do business with companies that align with their values and beliefs—and a whopping 83 percent of millennials say this.[1] Corporate responsibility is a big part of our purpose-driven culture, as should be the case with any organization. Reduced to an overly simplistic view of corporate responsibility, "doing good" is good for business. There is nothing in my 40-plus years of experience in corporate America that has ever indicated that profit and responsibility are incompatible. Of course, it is true that some companies put profit ahead of all else and that some leaders choose to disregard the well-being of their colleagues, but this is not how I have ever done business, and it is not an industry standard.

Setting the example of good corporate citizenship begins with individual leadership that ensures corporate responsibility is a substantial aspect of the company culture. I have to go back to my Aunt Millie here—watching her take her role in her community seriously profoundly influenced my thinking about how I and the companies I am part of operate worldwide. As I said, she participated in any way she could, ensuring elderly people received hot meals, facilitating a community center where people could connect, and even organizing political campaigns for candidates she believed in. She didn't have to do any of it, but she did it because she felt called to show her appreciation for being a citizen and a member of a community she loved and respected. That lesson has stayed with me. It means something.

That means that the crucial piece of this discussion is that the success of a responsible company starts at the personal and individual levels, with individual action and commitment. It is one of the most powerful ways to be heard. I have always been personally dedicated to using whatever influence I have to improve access to effective healthcare. This personal responsibility underpins all my decision-making. It's something all of us can practice. Everyone can make an effort around things they care about at work or in their community. Small stones make wide ripples. Encourage colleagues (and friends and family) to give back to their communities. There is so much you can do if you look.

> **Consistent, two-way communication is vital in critical situations, especially those directly affecting people's lives and livelihoods. Tell people what you know, what you don't know, and acknowledge that some things can only be revealed in time.**

To demonstrate the idea of caring, I try to take every opportunity possible to model responsibility around my values and concerns. Several colleagues and I signed on to run the Komen Connecticut Race for the Cure a few years ago. My initial goal was fairly modest: get 100 colleagues to commit to raising funds and help find a cure for breast cancer. Three years later, the running team had grown to more than 600. This event also allowed us to build camaraderie and do something meaningful together. Win-win. When team members see colleagues giving their time and committing to volunteerism and community, they tend to buy into the effort and see it as sincere. As a result, *they* want to engage and make a difference too. It's infectious in the best way. For a sense of how ingrained the spirit of giving back through volunteering is at Aetna and now CVS Health, since 2003, Aetna's team has contributed 2.5 million hours of volunteer work across the United States. Responsible and caring people who take action are successful people who build successful lives and businesses.

Think broadly. Go outside of your purview. How can you make a positive difference at work or in your community? Be open-minded about your opportunities and go where you are needed the most. Not only does this make a positive difference, it gives you a voice and elevates it. During the pandemic, I talked to a colleague on the board of directors of Marriott Hotels. The hospitality company had to furlough many workers during the time when many "nonessential" businesses were closed or minimized. While we were talking, the idea came up that perhaps CVS Health could hire some of those furloughed people temporarily. When the hotels were able to open back up, many of the people returned to their old jobs, and some stayed with us.

More importantly, we had a group of people who were open-minded enough to take on different jobs and learn new skills that they could bring back to their former jobs if they chose to. These new jobs included retail sales associates, distribution center professionals, pharmacy technicians, and customer service representatives. We helped many people who could have been financially hurt without work. It started with two people talking. Yes, we leveraged the unique positions we had, but this kind of thinking and problem solving can happen everywhere.

LEADERS ACT RESPONSIBLY TO ENSURE FUTURE ACCOUNTABILITY

Even if you are not in a position to initiate or facilitate big systemic changes, you can participate in projects that mean something to you and make an impact on your community.

A Family Commitment

One person can make a difference. There is much more openness today about mental health issues than when I was a young woman. Even less than 10 years ago, there was a great deal of reluctance to talk about it, let alone admit to having problems yourself or in your family. This is one of the reasons my husband, Kevin, founded the Quell Foundation to educate communities about issues and concerns surrounding mental health, promoting open, judgment-free dialogue. I am so proud of him for his support. The Quell Foundation strives to reduce the number of suicides, overdoses, and incarceration of people with mental illness. It encourages people to share their stories, increases access to mental health services, provides a pipeline of future mental healthcare professionals with scholarships, and trains first responders to recognize mental health crisis warning signs among their own. Since its founding, the Quell Foundation has awarded nearly $3 million in scholarships to 1,800 college and university students in 50 states.

Importance of Leadership and Colleague Resource Groups

We can all encourage team members to participate in employee resource groups around issues of importance to them. At one company, LGBTQ team members formed a group, and I participated in it as an ally. I firmly believe that such groups not only serve their team members by affirming their place in the company but also by helping the company innovate and grow in ways it might not otherwise have considered. After all, we serve all communities, as all communities need and deserve the best healthcare possible. Such was the case with this group. We talked about what could be done to enhance our business, advance our goals, and expand our customer base. Their idea was that the company should be known for supporting the LGBTQ community. My response was, "Great, how do we do that?" To which they replied, "A marketing campaign." So that is what we did: media, video, and a lot more. By 2015, when this took place, there were very few companies marketing directly to the LGBTQ community. We were not the first company or even the first insurance company to develop such a campaign, but we were certainly early adopters, and our credibility within the community was established.

Looking back now from just a few years' time, it is almost difficult to imagine why this could have been perceived as a controversial decision, since many companies that produce everything from breakfast cereals to automobiles specifically target the LGBTQ community in their advertising. Some team members did raise the question of whether such a bold move would alienate members of the public and perhaps cost us customers. A few customers did express their displeasure, but not to the extent that business was negatively affected. Nor did they have a negative effect on the company's reputation. The lesson in leadership here: when you act based on the company's core values, you stand on very firm ground.

That ground was deeply shaken in 2016 when a lone Islamic terrorist entered the Pulse nightclub in Orlando, Florida, intent on killing people, and he did. Forty-nine people were slaughtered, and 53 more were injured. Two of my team members were among the dead. This heinous hate crime remains the largest act of violence perpetrated against members of the gay community.

We marshaled our resources to help the families of the two team members killed in the attack, Christopher (Drew) Leinonen and Stanley Almodovar, and to help other team members traumatized by the event. We lowered the rainbow flag that flew over company headquarters and made counseling available to all team members. Indeed, we extended the resources of our employee assistance program to anyone who needed them.[2]

RESPONSIBILITY CAN MEAN MAKING TOUGH CALLS: VACCINE MANDATE

I had to make a decision in August 2021, as the COVID-19 Delta variant raged across the country: to mandate vaccines among all CVS Health employees or not. In every leader's career, there are times when unforeseen circumstances demand such decision-making, and you have to be ready for it. I had to determine whether to mandate vaccines for colleagues and if so, how to deal with any fallout or loss of talent. It has been proven that vaccines are effective, so I took a stand to save lives and established a safe workplace environment for all colleagues. I approved a policy requiring colleagues to be vaccinated with one of the three available vaccines. The vast majority of team members had already been vaccinated, so while the mandate applied to all colleagues, there were relatively few who still had not been vaccinated. In addition, vaccination would also be required of colleagues who worked in our corporate offices and all new hires. This was not a decision I took lightly. Still, after weighing the consequences, I had to stay on the side of the CDC's guidance to promote public and community health, particularly given we are a company doing all that is possible to promote public health.

Requiring vaccines as a condition of employment is one of those decisions that is uncomfortable to make because the consequences for some are so severe. I took no pleasure in that; however, my first allegiance as CEO is to make sure the company fulfills its corporate responsibility to maintain a safe workplace for everyone. It was in this context that I made the decision.

As it turned out, there was little fallout—most of the emails, letters, and phone calls I received about the decision were grateful in nature. Many people thanked me for taking this stand to create a safe workplace environment. I wasn't thinking about that when I made the decision because I'm not guided by what will be considered popular. However, it was gratifying to know that people supported that decision as a way to show our trust in the science to help the country turn the corner on the devastation of the pandemic. You may be called to make hard choices and stand by your decision—make sure they are well-thought-out. Weigh the pros and cons and understand and accept the consequences. Your voice will be heard. Personal responsibility is a powerful currency. Don't squander it—you've got it, use it!

REMEMBER THIS:

► **Personal responsibility is a powerful way to show you care.** Get involved in programs and policies that help causes that are allied with your interests, your goals, and your industry.

► **Walk the talk.** If you want others to do something, you have to be willing to do it yourself. That means volunteering alongside colleagues and team members who are in the community and engaging with it, rolling up your sleeves in tough times, and stepping into roles outside of your job description when necessary.

► **Everyone has access to personal responsibility.** There is great power and influence in acting responsibly. It gives you credibility and "go-to" status professionally and personally.

9

Care Sees Us Through Crisis

Understand what can be at stake before a crisis occurs.

"I want to handle this," I told my CEO. The pandemic had hit one year into the biggest healthcare acquisition in a decade, CVS Health acquiring Aetna. I asked for the assignment to co-lead the COVID-19 Executive Task Force during the first few days of the pandemic when the world was shutting down while I remained president for Aetna. The company had no senior executives leading crisis situations. My philosophy is to raise your hand if you can make a difference. Don't stay on the sidelines. I volunteered to jump in and spearhead the coordination effort. This is just the kind of work I love, and it was so important. I knew we would be successful.

My prior experiences with hurricanes and other severe weather events gave me the insight to bring multiple groups together to address an event without a playbook. I had been down the natural disaster road before. In 2018, I led Aetna through two successful hurricane response efforts. I knew the importance of planning for the longer term, establishing a crisis structure, and implementing a comprehensive communication plan. I'm not going to say it wasn't chaotic in the beginning— it was because the company had not worked together across all lines of business like this before. However, we quickly got organized, scaled our response, and started making a huge impact. It was a massive undertaking. My offer was accepted, and I moved forward to tackle a project no one had coordinated before, during a crisis most people had never experienced firsthand—and for the entire company. It tested everything I knew about leadership.

No one walks into work saying today's the day a global crisis will occur. We knew a pandemic could happen; there has been a great deal of predictive analysis of the likelihood of a global pandemic for decades,[1] and we had strategies for dealing with various eventualities tied to such a catastrophe. That's one reason why our supply chain for our CVS pharmacies didn't break down: We rolled out testing and vaccination sites efficiently, maintained high levels of medication and product inventory, and stayed open to support customers, patients, and members. Across our other lines of business, we expanded benefit coverage policies to ensure we minimized gaps in care for patients and ramped up our capability to provide virtual health services. Still, there were surprises that we had to tackle.

Things happened very quickly after that. Our highly capable infectious disease clinical team was running our virus planning and response efforts. Still, we needed many parts of the company to cooperate and act collaboratively to make our response as effective as possible. It was quickly announced that my colleague and peer, the chief medical officer, would run the clinical side of our response effort while I co-led the executive task force from an operations standpoint. CVS Health serves over 100 million people as a health insurer and pharmacy benefits manager, over 90 million people as a pharmacy, and over 50 million customers digitally. We had no other alternative but to get it right. We had to help team members and customers move from anxiety and fear to hope.

I personally reached out to our top 20 customers; other executives connected with our top 200 customers. Within the first 48 hours of forming the team, we restricted all company travel and canceled attendance at all large meetings and conferences for the foreseeable future. We made the decision that team members work from home. Within a week, we got about 70 percent of the corporate workforce set up for remote work, and that percentage increased over the following week. It was a huge feat because of the equipment and technology needed. Most of our call centers were transitioned to home-based. Only distribution center personnel, transportation professionals, retail store team members, and pharmacists—all frontline workers—were on location along with a small number of corporate staff needed to keep our operations running. I am humbled by these women and men and how they rose to the occasion, came to work every day, and provided needed services to customers, especially during the early days of the pandemic when there were so many uncertainties.

During the first weekend that COVID-19 emerged as a very real threat to the safety of Americans, we had already started to notice what items seemed to be selling out more quickly than normal, including vitamins, toilet paper, paper towels, soap, rubbing alcohol, and hand sanitizer—all the products that have since become iconic symbols of our collective panic.

Coordination and speed were key. We had to assemble teams from across the company—management, technicians, clinicians, sales, finance, customer service, and others. Before that selection process even began, I framed our crisis and business response by establishing four guiding principles: protect the health and safety of team members, meet the health needs of customers, maintain business continuity, and anticipate marketplace dynamics and needs. We could not close our CVS locations—they were essential. We needed to make equal access to needed care a priority for colleagues and customers. And we had to continue looking around corners to see innovations we needed to develop, which included in-store testing, mass tents to accommodate demand, pop-up clinics, and virtual primary care.

When confronting challenges, think through events and situations as holistically as possible. How do we think about this as a company? Where do we want to be when this is over, and how do we get there? There are so many actions leaders can take to sustain the business and respond to challenges if you frame decisions around who needs what the most. Within 48 hours, we set up a COVID-19 response infrastructure, representing key areas of the company to address the critical issues involved in ensuring we could continue operations safely and effectively serve our customers and clients. I first had to decide which parts of the organization needed to be at the table and who the best people were to represent those interests. How do we find the best people to create the strongest teams, and how do we keep up with what is happening in the United States and the world while maintaining business continuity? This process accelerated the integration of the two company cultures—CVS Health and Aetna—and brought together individuals who otherwise would not have been thought about in tandem.

Meeting with these teams twice daily, morning and afternoon, we established new policies and waived some existing ones. We immediately liberalized as many relevant policies as possible on the insurance side to ensure there were no gaps in care for patients. We offered access to virtual care visits with zero copays—the first insurance company in the nation to do so. On the CVS retail side, we offered free delivery for prescriptions for 90 days because we didn't want people to go to the store if they didn't have to. We waived 30-day refill restrictions and allowed patients to fill 90-day prescriptions to ensure they continued taking their medication while many states were shut down. We covered the cost of daycare for our frontline team members and awarded them bonuses. These policy shifts went a long way toward ensuring the health and safety of our workforce, alleviating our customers' own potential health crises, and streamlined our ability to serve clients.

We developed a process to work together and side by side. It was fascinating and resulted in an incredible learning curve. The key strategies for success never change, even with something as new as this response: listening to team members and customers, checking in, owning accountability, innovating, collaborating, and learning what we didn't know while taking action. It all came together. The people we temporarily pulled out of their jobs to work on the COVID-19 response resulted in incredible development opportunities. Everyone rose to the occasion, and we identified leadership talent.

We also had to work with local, state, and federal governments and the pharmaceutical companies developing the vaccines, which presented other coordination challenges. There were differences between what the states wanted and how the federal government wanted to handle situations. During the government's Operation Warp Speed initiative, we met weekly with the government's COVID-19 Task Force, sharing with it our principal assets of CVS locations and our scheduling and distribution methods for getting vaccines into long-term care facilities. We collaborated with them to do something that had never been done before. This speaks to the importance of public-private relationships in addressing the United States' biggest public health crisis.

We moved quickly to secure masks and other personal protective equipment for our frontline colleagues and to install plexiglass shields in our stores to offer what we believed at the time would be a protective barrier for them and our customers. We monitored the medication and over-the-counter product supply chain closely and put processes in place to deal with the eventuality of shortages. Teams continuously looked for alternative products and services we can carry in the store should we encounter difficulties in procuring certain items. We became doubly conscious of this process during the pandemic. There was no finger pointing or passing blame along. No crumpling papers and throwing them on tables. We worked together toward solutions. One included liberalized insurance coverage policies to expand access to health services and closed gaps in care for over half a million people through Aetna who could not get in to see a doctor.

We also had to be proactive about the health fallouts that were side effects of shelter-in-place rules. We had to help keep our customers' mental health strong. We knew some, if not many, of the people facing isolation due to stay-at-home guidance would suffer greatly. We opened a 24-hour nurse line nationally, but the mental health piece must also be addressed. We had experience with this since hurricanes cause extreme stress, and we'd handled the mental health aspect of disaster relief in the past. We set up special hotlines so anyone—it didn't matter if you were a CVS customer—could call and talk to someone. It was effective—people did use the system and were helped by it.

In terms of vaccine distribution management, before the rollout, we felt we needed to go into the details one by one: What are the known potential side effects? What are the protocols for administering the available vaccines? Transportation, storage, and refrigeration issues were top of mind, given that the vaccines must be kept at specific temperatures to maintain efficacy. Disposal was an issue for medical waste and unused, expired vaccines. Quality control was paramount. It was a relay race. Not only did we have to understand how distribution would function, but we also had to work closely with manufacturers and with the federal government. We had to develop and innovate digital tools for scheduling appointments correctly.

Finally, we were ready to invite a general from the US Army who was helping to lead the federal government's pandemic response to look at our distribution center and learn about our plans to get the vaccines to locations all across the country. The general walked in wearing his green khakis, a team of his people following behind him. That his presence took over the room is an understatement.

The general toured our crisis center and we showed him the logistics required to get the vaccines to nationwide locations, explaining how vaccine administration would be done safely and efficiently in large parking lots and other open areas. We also had to revolutionize our digital capabilities so people could schedule online. That was a big innovation for us.

It was complicated planning and action done quickly. The general was impressed and, that day, walked out of the room saying, "CVS is ready." I am both proud and humbled that we were able to pitch in and help during this unprecedented crisis.

The coordination between teams from across the two merged companies accelerated the integration of CVS Health. We got to know each other and each other's businesses. A crisis like this makes people drop all pretense, and any skepticism or trust issues have to fall away if you are going to accomplish anything. If I could name any silver lining from this national and global crisis, it would be the formation of tightly woven teams that inspired those around them to stand up and take part in solving big problems.

Even during a pandemic, it is important to remember that healthcare is local. We were one of the first COVID-19 testing sites in the United States, established in Shrewsbury, Massachusetts, on a blustery day, a long line of tents set up, with an even longer line of cars filled with people waiting to be tested.

The pandemic and our response also exposed critical gaps in healthcare. We purchased vans and put them in underserved communities with no CVS location nearby and no large accessible areas where people in cars could gather in order for those in more urban communities to access vaccines and testing.

Like all businesses, CVS Health faced an unexpected and potentially catastrophic event for our company, team members, customers, and clients during the COVID-19 pandemic. It was an event that tested leaders in unpredictable ways. We are still trying to understand the long-term impact the shutdown will ultimately have on our industry, society, the economy, and overall mental and physical health. The many unknowns means that our crisis planning and strategy around COVID-19 will continue as more data emerges and economic and social shifts evolve.

It took many people and many hours to figure out all the paths we needed to be on to get the rollout right. It was an extraordinary process, and everyone, at every level and department of the organization, pulled together.

Once we learned that broad vaccination was the only way we could hope to achieve normalcy, we were proactive. Once the Delta variant became an issue in mid-2021, we realized that vaccination rates needed to be higher than they were. We already offered free vaccines to anyone who wanted one, but we needed more people to get vaccinated. By the time Delta raged through various communities, too many people had fallen into a false sense of security that COVID-19 was going away. It wasn't. The vaccines provided strong efficacy.

We were determined to come out better and stronger for the pandemic. Our entire management team and I went into stores as we rolled out vaccine distribution, registered people, and guided them through the process. I didn't want to ask anyone to do anything I wouldn't do, so it was important to show CVS colleagues, our onsite clinicians, and pharmacists that all levels of the company were with them. We worked alongside the CVS retail team members so we could see with our own eyes what was happening in communities. I remember one elderly customer who walked into one of our CVS locations asking to be vaccinated. The teams had set up the scheduling process digitally and asked this customer to return home and use a computer or other device to schedule an appointment for another day. This was a good learning experience for all of us. We had set up what we thought was a seamless process to schedule all vaccination appointments digitally and had not considered the process or flow if people walked in without an appointment, given all the strict COVID protocols in place. I walked this customer to the pharmacy and helped set him up and get ready to receive the vaccine. I intervened and used this as a coaching moment for our team to be ready to pivot if needed and adapt to a customer's needs and situation. Sometimes rules are made to be broken.

Some people's instinct might be to run away from a crisis . . . but I run to them. Raise your hand and volunteer. Share your wisdom if you have special knowledge that you may not use at work but would be helpful in emergency planning. Help organize—be willing to do anything when pitching in. Reliable, calm, and capable people are noticed and heard during a crisis. You also learn a great deal from this kind of work, and you often partner with colleagues you may not cross paths with in your day-to-day role. While no one wants crises in life or work, they are inevitable. When they happen, they offer an opportunity for you to rise to the occasion and make a difference—take up space at the table.

A crisis requires people involved to drop all pretense, and any skepticism or trust issues have to fall away if you are going to accomplish anything.

EXPERIENCE READIES YOU
FOR THE UNEXPECTED

I've experienced many challenges over the decades, personally and professionally. Observation and account-ability are two recurring themes in this book, and that's no exception in a crisis. These qualities are vital when dealing with acute and time-sensitive challenges. From the start of my career, I have kept a keen eye on how those with leadership directives navigated worst-case scenar-ios and guided people toward best-case outcomes. Some rose to the occasion and succeeded, while I saw others falter and fail. Seeing the behaviors that produced the best results (and the worst) offered insight into how to handle emergencies, so when I was faced with leading a team out of a crisis, I had some guidance.

Managing any crisis well is not just about making a series of quick decisions to mitigate what's happening. Don't mistake that for leading through a crisis. It takes engagement well beforehand to foresee the events that could negatively affect your business—and prepare for them. While contingency planning is a mandate of lead-ership, you have to be flexible and agile because events can and will happen before, during, and after a crisis that are not in your control and will not be predicted by even the most seasoned crisis management strategists.

The best responses to a crisis move you forward. They make your business better and stronger. The bad ones add to the disruption and create weaknesses in morale and response. Positive strategies that apply to challenges large and small include assessing the issue so the size of your response matches the scope of the problem; imposing order on chaos through smart delegation; acting swiftly and decisively but not hurriedly; managing the expectations of those around you; demonstrating composure and control; listening and learning; and staying flexible but focused. Set direction, pull back to gain perspective, take a long view, don't get too caught up in everyday decisions, and communicate. Measure results. Pivot when necessary.

Consistency is important; everybody has to feel like they're in the same boat going in the same direction because without a sense of purpose-driven unity, disaster response falls apart quickly, especially in large companies with disparate offices and operations. You want to be part of the solution in a crisis; everyone has a part to play.

Finally, in a crisis be transparent, tell your team what you know. Share information. Anyone can have important information and insights in a crisis, so share what you know and open the door to allow the experiences of others into the conversation. This is one of my guiding principles, my North Star, if you will. When you are honest in this way, you build trust and commitment during a crisis. I want my team to trust that I will use that information wisely, for their benefit and that of the company.

The philosophy that I espouse is to tell your team what you know, what you don't know, what you need to know, and that you know other information that you cannot share right now but will share when you are able.

LISTENING IS A GO-TO STRATEGY

Don't ignore the small problems because they can become big issues before you know it. I want to catch problems early and fast. Listen to your people. We look across the company to see what's happening, identify potential trouble spots and issues, and act on them. Focusing on detail and closeness to the customer also offers unique insights that help us get ahead of the curve and stop a problem before it worsens.

As I've mentioned, customer sentiment is one data point I always look at. It is an excellent barometer of where problems are located. I received an email from a customer who said that he had been on hold with our customer service for one hour. I took this complaint seriously and did not ignore it as a one-off. It's unacceptable for customers to hold on the phone for an hour. Everyone's time is valuable. What the heck was going on? Did it signal a systemic problem?

I picked up the phone immediately after reading the email. I called the head of operations to ask if this customer's experience was a fluke or if it was a symptom of a technical issue with our phone systems and call center. It turned out we had recently gone through a telephone systems conversion, and phone operations had been down for a few hours; there were glitches that kept people from reaching us and those that kept people on hold for unacceptably long wait times. He knew about the problem, was monitoring it, and ultimately was able to correct it. Unfortunately, it was not done in time to help this particular customer. My philosophy is to treat customers like family members or loved ones. We reached out to him, let him know about the problem, apologized, and got him the assistance he needed—later than I would have liked, but we did follow through.

Continually improve and practice plans to make sure they work. When changing systems or making technical updates, consider how to prevent or mitigate problems during these transitions when technicians are working. Being prepared means considering scenarios that include all the things that could go wrong so your team can develop mitigating actions around them. Every small problem is an opportunity to make processes work better. If you look at obstacles and challenges in this way, solving small annoyances becomes part of the mission of continuous improvement and can prevent larger issues later on.

Not all crises involve external events, such as bad weather, pandemics, cyberattacks, civil unrest, and so on. Sometimes a crisis happens internally because company structure or protocol changes were not handled well. These scenarios require the same planning as natural disasters and other unpredictable forms of chaos in order to avoid backlash and destructive confusion among team members and customers.

THE BEST-LAID PLANS: NATURAL DISASTERS

One kind of crisis everyone should be prepared for is severe weather—and make no mistake, this leadership skill can and will require that you use your voice as you take up space at the table. Dealing with these natural disasters prepared me to tackle our pandemic response. Two places where hurricanes and nor'easters are part of life are New England and Florida, locations I am familiar with, so I know personally how to be ready regarding what supplies I need to have on hand. This kind of personal and family preparation is translatable to larger-scale planning, and there is more correlation between personal and group planning for natural disasters than you might think. The leadership aspect of responding well to acute weather events, skills useful in many scenarios, demonstrates your presence of mind and ability to act quickly, work collaboratively, and prepare properly.

Severe weather events are generally localized or regional. While these kinds of crises do not affect every part of a multilocation company, a breakdown in transportation or supply lines can reverberate well beyond the location of a storm, so preparation for natural disasters has to be both specific to the affected area and to a certain degree, the response must be company-wide.

Every business leader should do mock disaster recovery so there is some practice before a real event occurs. This might seem obvious, but I mention it because you learn as you go. The more you anticipate, the stronger and more effective your response will be when the time comes to act.

All the organizations I have worked for have designated a disaster leader, a person or team that becomes a hub for the constant stream of information coming from the field. Everyone needs to know what's going on. Taking a disciplined approach is key if that is you—and why not volunteer to be part of this work? Learn from past weather events and responses. How do we keep the business running the best that we can? How do we keep people employed? How do we serve our customers and communities? Create a playbook based on the answers. Assemble a team, and engage all parts of the company, including communications and public relations.

> **While no one wants crises in life or work, they are inevitable. When they happen, they offer an opportunity for you to rise to the occasion and make a difference—take up space and speak up.**

In August 2021, Hurricane Ida was approaching Louisiana. I had dealt with numerous severe weather events throughout my professional life, so I knew what to do based on experience. Our reaction to the impending storm summarizes our process in these circumstances: I contacted the head of crisis management to ensure we were preparing for it correctly. Operations had already begun positioning trucks in the state to ensure supplies could be delivered to affected areas. We were also prepared for power outages in terms of keeping team members and physical locations safe and secure. We had a transportation plan to ensure our team members could access safe locations with power.

My learning in this area started early. In the early 2000s, I was president of a dental business. That business was located in Florida. In 2004, four hurricanes touched down in the Sunshine State over a six-week period. Charley, Frances, Ivan, and Jeanne roared through—some touched the west coast, while others devastated the east coast. Central Florida was not spared either. Frances and Jeanne hit almost the exact same spot on the east coast of Florida, in Plantation, near Fort Lauderdale. Jeanne was a major hurricane that added to the severe damage already done by Frances, and it was the final straw. The city had to shut down. There were fallen trees everywhere, and no electricity or gas available at the pump. All of this meant there was little capacity for transportation to get through.

While I was not directly overseeing recovery, I was on daily calls with the people on the ground and with the operations folks who were managing response and recovery. I was up north, in our corporate headquarters, and was deeply frustrated by feeling so helpless. I remember talking to my head of operations during Hurricane Jeanne. She was on her cellphone in her bathroom, in the center of her house, waiting for the storm to pass. We talked for as long as we could, and I reassured her, but at a certain point, everything went down. I had no communications with anyone for a period of time.

A few days after the storm, electricity still was out and people were in need. I'd had enough of waiting. I asked permission to charter a private plane to fly to Florida. Once I had the go-ahead, I filled the plane from floor to ceiling with everything I thought our people might need, from bottled water to dry goods. I made it to the office, where I was able to reach out via a call chain; I called a list of key people to relay information, and they each had a list of people to call, and so on. This is how we let our colleagues know we had supplies. It took time to coordinate and distribute what we had brought, but as with all crises, my guiding principles drove the effort and my commitment to seeing it through. Leaders put the health and safety of team members first, to protect them and enable them to serve their communities. After that, you can focus on preserving the health and safety of customers, clients, and communities. Finally, this enables you to maintain business continuity.

When superstorm Sandy hit in October 2012, it devastated much of the northeastern United States. So many people were displaced, including many of my team members and colleagues. Why not book a block of hotel rooms wherever we could in the general area of the storm damage? It was important that our people were safe and secure. We found temporary housing for our colleagues who lost everything in the storm. We needed to get our colleagues in affected areas out of harm's way. That went a long way with our people.

Leaders put the health and safety of team members first, to protect them and enable them to serve their communities. After that you can focus on preserving the health and safety of customers, clients, and communities.

I knew that something simple like a hotel room would be important because a few years earlier we had seen the effect it had on team members during another devastating storm. In 2016 a communications colleague was one of the many team members who received a hotel room during another terrible weather event—for 10 days. "It was a lifesaver," she told me. "At home, we had only a single gas fireplace that we were using to try and generate enough heat for my family of five and my mother. Six of us were sleeping in sleeping bags in front of the fireplace. It was absolutely miserable, and there were no hotels to be found anywhere. Then, suddenly, my company had a room for us. It was amazing for the whole family. You don't forget things like that," she said of the experience. After this storm, securing blocks of rooms became part of our routine response planning for serious weather events.

We have worked diligently to create a company culture that is sensitive to team members in crisis. We make an effort to do what I call a "walk-around" to check in with how everyone is doing in the regions that are predicted to be affected. In 2017, Hurricane Harvey touched down in Texas and Louisiana and brought a great deal of destruction, catastrophic flooding, and more than 100 deaths. One of our market presidents told me about a team member who needed milk for her baby and cash for other necessary provisions. She had neither. He found a way to get to her house to bring her milk and money out of his own pocket. That behavior speaks to the strength of purpose, culture, and community we have built. These fuel everyday productivity but they also inspire people to be their best in a crisis.

I was deeply impressed by that local team; they were doing anything and everything they could both as a group and individually to help their colleagues. Harvey was an unusual storm. Most hurricanes and nor'easters shut things down for a day or two, maybe three. But the damage from Harvey lasted weeks. Seeing the efforts of team members helped us consider new ways of responding to disasters. It resulted in a policy to provide cash to team members who needed it. It was an idea that initially met with resistance but one that I insisted upon because it was the right thing to do. It was also low cost; we were not giving large sums to individuals, just small amounts of $100 to $200 to get people through. We figured out a simple distribution system and a way to keep track of the expenditure. It wasn't that complicated.

This kind of caring and whatever-it-takes attitude does not develop the day before a storm rolls in; it is something that grows over time, consistently. It's part of giving people permission to do the right thing, which is often lacking in corporate structures. Seeing how my colleagues responded was a reassuring confirmation of a cultural shift I saw as the fairly new president of Aetna at the time. I think people saw that the company was acting in a new way.

Trust is the most important thing in a crisis: people have to have faith in how the crisis is being led, and conversely, leadership has to trust that team members will do the right thing. So many companies build procedures around that 0.5 percent of people who are going to abuse the system versus the 99.5 percent who will respect it. If you are involved in making policy or advocating for it, whether it's crisis management or anything else, go with the 99.5 percent. If you find out that 0.5 percent ripped you off, take the loss and identify them. Deal with the problem. But do not build your organization's policies and processes around a minority of those who may not be team players. Create a culture where most are. Advocate for policies for most people, and show that the loyalty and enthusiasm these approaches engender far outweigh the costs.

REMEMBER THIS:

► **Be someone who sees and fixes problems when they're small.** Don't let seemingly minor issues go unaddressed. If you see something, take the lead and say something. Offer solutions. It's less expensive and easier to repair minimal damage than it is to wait to act until an issue becomes significant.

► **Be flexible and agile.** Understand that the best-laid emergency plans are based on common scenarios that have happened in the past and that current events don't always play out the way you've predicted. Be willing to shift and pivot when necessary.

► **Advocate for policies around the majority of people in your organization.** Don't let a small percentage of team members who take advantage of situations determine the rules for everyone else.

The Power of Purpose and Choice

You control your own destiny.
Use that power to make a difference.

I remember it like it was yesterday: a beautiful summer day on the Cape (Cape Cod, Massachusetts) in the early 1980s. I was working at a local restaurant, which required me to wear a classic New England Colonial uniform–looking cotton floral dress with puffed sleeves, fitted bodice, and gathered skirt, along with an apron and a matching bonnet. It was one of those typical New England summer jobs hundreds of high school and college kids did to earn money over seasonal breaks. Ever thinking of the future, I never let anyone take a picture of me in that get-up, knowing it would come back to haunt me later in life. Good thing cell phone cameras weren't around back then. Kevin actually worked at the same restaurant, and he's the only one I know personally who has seen me in my Colonial gear. The hourly wage wasn't high, but the summer crowds were usually pretty good, meaning tips could be lucrative.

One day, several college-age men came in and ordered lunch. After finishing their meal, they strolled out of the diner without paying. This scam has many terms, including dining and dashing. At any rate, I saw exactly what they had done, and breaking protocol—because you're not supposed to actually confront customers who don't pay—I ran after them into the parking lot, hoping to grab at least one by his collar. Both were lean and a lot taller than I was. I was so enraged that someone would try to get away with not paying for a meal (especially one I had served them); neither the rules nor the size difference mattered to me. I was mad.

I managed to catch one of the guys and dragged him back into the restaurant, with his friend following sheepishly behind. The only reason why I think he complied with me was that he was in shock that this tiny young woman in a prairie dress and a bonnet was actually chasing him through a parking lot and quick enough to grab hold of him. By the time we had returned to the restaurant, my manager had called the police. When they arrived on the scene, one of the officers said to the pair that they better pay their bill or else he would arrest them. They came up with the money (I recall a lot of pocket change was involved). As they were turning to leave, one of the officers said to them, "What about her tip?" as he tilted his head in my direction. That's when one of the guys reluctantly retrieved a five-dollar bill from his pocket and threw it at me. I caught it and stuffed it in my apron pocket. A caveat: I would *not* do this today, and I don't recommend this response if you are in a similar situation. It was a different era, and I let my frustration at their appalling behavior get the better of me.

I share this story because taking up space and using your voice for doing what's right is something I will always stand by. I admit to having a strong sense of justice and the personal philosophy that you won't mess with me. That has served me well over the years. I might have been a petite young college student, often aloof with colleagues and sometimes reticent to trust, but I was and am a fighter—for myself and others. People underestimate me. That's a mistake. If people underestimate you, use it to your advantage. The element of surprise works no matter who you are—or what you are wearing.

I have learned over the years that we *do* control our own destinies. Where we go does not depend on where we start from, as long as we strive to be the best we can be and do what we know is just. Look at my experience: I came from "any-Ware" and ended up leading one of the largest companies in the world (in the top 10 on the Fortune 500 list[1]), despite the barriers I faced along the way. We all have the ability to do what we want to do in life. Write your own story; don't let anyone else get in the way of that. Listen to criticism; absorb what sounds useful and discard what doesn't. Be accountable. We all experience bumps on the road. Happiness, joy, and balance are worthy pursuits and give you the strength to be heard when you come to the table. Making time to decompress, exercise, relax, and have fun are so important as you build a career. How you choose to spend your time, and with whom, are critical to your well-being too. Take care of your health; prioritize it. Your health should never be something you take care of on the weekend or when you have time—because you never have time unless you make it a priority.

There is no direct route to your aspirations or a "correct" path to follow. Everyone comes into their own and succeeds in their own way. Achieving your dreams is a combination of drawing on your interests and using your personal style to work hard, stay persistent, find supporters and champions, cultivate healthy relationships, take care of yourself, and maintain your curiosity, drive, and ambition. It's quite a recipe, but one that anyone can use despite the rate of change in business, the marketplace, and technology.

It doesn't matter what happens tomorrow, or in 5 or 10 years. The themes in this book—accountability, vulnerability, authenticity, integrity, equity in all things, strategic risk, active listening, and genuine diversity—are, as far as I'm concerned, tried and true. They will work for you, no matter what the future holds or how the tides turn. Stay alert and accountable, embrace change, and see around corners as much as you can, and you will weather the future just fine.

> We *do* control our own destiny. Where we go does not depend on where we start from, as long as we strive to be the best we can be and do what we know is just.

EMBRACING MY PURPOSE

As much as there is trepidation about what is coming next in healthcare, the corporate world, society, and culture, there is a lot to be excited about. Healthcare will become more personalized in terms of the medicines you take and the care you receive. Your health information will be connected that gives you vital insights real-time on your mobile device. It's happening right now. You will have more power and autonomy over your healthcare than ever before: people with chronic health conditions will be able to connect their doctors so they can easily communicate with each other. You will have more reliable information so you can make better decisions about your own health. That's good news.

I do think it is important, as I have said throughout this book, to take a stand on something that is important to you. It doesn't have to be healthcare, but I use it as an example here because it's my *why*—why I chose my career path. For me, the work I do is only meaningful if I can make a difference to ensure that everyone who wants access to quality healthcare, has it and gets what is appropriate and necessary for them. My purpose, and the purpose my colleagues align around, is to bring our heart to every moment of health. Our focus is on improving health. It's good business to care about health equity, especially for those in vulnerable communities. That means increasing opportunities for everyone to live the healthiest life possible, no matter who they are, how old they are, what they look like, where they live, or how much money they make. My interest in health equity is a product of seeing firsthand how lack of access to health information and services devastated my family. We had limited access to care, and the people around me, in my neighborhood and community, had limited access. Very rarely did any of us, my siblings and I, go to a doctor or a dentist. We went when there was an acute problem to be solved, not for health management. Regular care might have helped my mother.

Chronic health conditions like obesity, diabetes, heart disease, smoking, and substance abuse are all factors in our collective health. They were problems I witnessed growing up and continued to see as I followed my career path. One of the critical ways we're now trying to address these issues and others is by understanding the social determinants of health, which are the conditions in which people are born, grow, live, work, and age. They are mostly responsible for health inequities.[2]

Across the United States (and the globe) gaps in health are large, persistent, and in many cases, increasingly caused by barriers at all levels of society. It's hard to be healthy without access to good jobs, schools, and safe, affordable homes—all reasons CVS Health makes an effort to contribute to robust access to jobs that pay well, communities that are safe, and housing that is affordable.

It may seem counterintuitive for someone who is guiding one of the top healthcare companies in the United States, one with more than 300,000 colleagues and multiple consumer and corporate interests, to talk about health equity and the benefits of having solutions at the community level. It can be easy to forget who you are serving when you are in such an environment—individuals— and this fact is something that I remind myself of daily. But health is personal and it is local. Remembering and catering to the individual person-to-person moments is what can help all companies, regardless of size, survive and thrive in an increasingly globalized and impersonal technology-driven world.

> **Curating small person-to-person moments can help all leaders survive and thrive in an increasingly globalized and impersonal technology-driven world.**

YOU HAVE THE POWER

Right before the pandemic, one of the last public events I did was at my middle school, where I met with children. I brought my dog, and together "we" read a story to the kids and talked to them about careers and choices. It was a wonderful personal moment that probably brought me more joy than the kids, although they loved it too. Here I was, a kid from Ware, coming back to meet some of the future leaders and voices in my hometown. And yes, many of our most effective voices will come from towns just like Ware all over the US and the world. The kids all sent me thank-you notes afterward, and I treasure every one of them.

For me, it was a chance to offer some words of encouragement to these young people—and I thank them for that opportunity. We do not realize the power of that old chestnut—*if I can do it, so can you*—has on children and adults alike who may feel they lack a voice or a place at the table of influence. It was a powerful moment to step back and offer these words of encouragement. There were many children who were just like me in that classroom. One, in particular, a young lady who was petrified to tell me her name, struck a chord. I think about her often and hope she finds her voice and the opportunity to do amazing things.

Should she choose one, her career path will likely not be linear. But truth be told, your career path will probably not be that linear either. Detours will happen. Life will happen. And your current plans may not pan out—or you might revise them along the way. When I graduated from college, I could never have envisioned myself in the space I am in now. If someone asked me my ultimate career goal, I probably would not have answered "CEO of a company ranked in the top 10 largest on the Fortune 500." It would not have even occurred to me that this was possible. But it *is* possible if it's what you want. You have a chance to take up space at every table you want to join.

REMEMBER THIS:

► **Seek out personal interactions.** Find ways to connect personally with colleagues, customers, and the community. These special moments—whether it's a one-on-one check-in with a colleague or a visit to a local school to give the class a pep talk—remind us that we are human and part of something bigger than ourselves.

► **Take up space at the table; then create space for someone else.** Use the strategies and stories you've absorbed in this book to use your voice and help others who may be unfairly underrated or underrepresented to use their voices alongside you.

► **Write your own takeaways.** Note what resonated with you in this book and from others who share their experience and wisdom. What is meaningful to you? How can you apply it to your goals and aspirations, your passions and obsessions? It's time to get to work.

CONCLUSION

've shared my story; now it is time to bring *your* story to life. The skills I've talked about in this book will help you choose to take up space:

▶ **Be engaged.** Show an interest in colleagues and projects. Say yes to opportunities even if they don't seem to align with your passions and ambitions. The skills you learn from accepting challenges no one else wants can lead to big goals and new, important assignments.

▶ **Show your strength through your vulnerability.** Don't be afraid to be authentic. I'm not talking about complaining or revealing a lot of personal information. Rather, be honest about your concerns and challenges.

▶ **Own your past to define a better future.** I learned this lesson early in my career and promised myself not to allow my sorrows to dictate my future. Eventually, I had to open up about my past—and in many ways, I wish I had done it sooner. It was liberating to talk about my childhood trauma and to show how it was intricately connected to my passion for health care. It was a powerful way to enlist others in the mission to make healthcare better and more accessible to more people.

▶ **Don't let your emotional baggage weigh you down.** Once you have acknowledged past hurts and disappointments, let them go. Don't let it drag down your enthusiasm.

▶ **Let everyone sing in their range.** While you should not be intimidated from using your unique voice, give others the same grace and space to use their distinct way of expressing their best selves. Encourage it and them!

▶ **Your path is never linear.** Don't become discouraged when goals seem out of reach, or the road has many detours. Those alternate routes and side streets add to your experience and understanding of the "big picture." They make you stronger, more agile, and more adaptable—all key skills in the twenty-first century.

▶ **Learn by doing.** Nothing beats experience when it comes to knowledge building. Ask questions, observe, and take every opportunity to learn about your industry and things you're interested in outside of work.

▶ **Lead with empathy.** I never want to lose my humanity at work or in life. I am just the people we serve, and my teammates, colleagues, and I have more in common than differences. Find common ground; it's a good way to build empathy. Take opportunities to walk in someone else's shoes. Listen to learn, not to answer.

▶ **Focus on your health.** Well-being is so important to individuals but also to communities. We cannot help others if we don't help ourselves. There are so many resources today to help you pursue good health. We still have a lot of work to do regarding access and equity in health care, and I hope I can make a difference in this way. But we all have a responsibility to ensure we eat well, get fresh air, and exercise. We need to ask for help when we need it, especially regarding our mental health. Become an advocate for yourself.

▶ **Take up space and use your voice.** The most important parting advice I can offer. You deserve it. And then create space for someone else.

ACKNOWLEDGMENTS

Writing a book about the lessons you have learned throughout your life is a surreal process. I'm forever grateful for Karen Kelly, my writing partner, for her keen insight and ongoing support in bringing my stories to life.

Kevin Lynch: You gave me the courage to share my personal stories that have shaped who I am today. Thank you for your unending patience in reading all of the drafts with me!

Kathi Lucey: One of my dearest friends who lived with me through most of these experiences. You always pushed me to break through barriers, overcome obstacles, and keep blazing a path forward.

Carrah Kalat, Laurie Havanec, Paula Branco: Your support, friendship, and honesty throughout the review process was extraordinary. Thank you for reading early drafts and helping me with so many of the stories that we shared.

Katerina Guerraz: Your insights, candor, thought partnership, and encouragement throughout this process have been instrumental.

For my family: Jim, Cheryl, and Monica. You cheered me on throughout this incredible journey. Each of you sustained me in ways that I never knew that I needed. I am so thankful to have you in my life.

Jim Stewart and Peter Baltren: While both have passed away, they played a critical role that started in the early part of my life and career. They saw something in me and continued to encourage me to have big dreams.

Bob Hughes, who stood beside me throughout my entire career and challenged me to do better. He pushed me to overcome the self-doubt that at times would surface.

Kathryn Metcalfe: Your dedication, support, and review of the early drafts were critical for ensuring the lessons of each story came through.

Special thanks to Casey Ebro, the ever-patient executive editor and my agent, Carol Mann.

All of the mentors, sponsors, and colleagues who inspired me along the way. Every interaction and word of encouragement stayed with me and continues to shape me as a leader, colleague, and person.

NOTES

CHAPTER 2

1. https://www.modernhealth care.com/article/20180606
   /NEWS/180609948/cvs-health-chooses-aetna-executives
   -to-stay-post-merger

CHAPTER 3

1. https://www.kff.org/coronavirus-COVID-19/issue-brief
   /the-implications-of-COVID-19-for-mental-health-and
   -substance-use/
2. CDC WISQARS Leading Causes of Death Report. https://
   wisqars.cdc.gov/data/lcd/home
3. CDC WISQARS Leading Causes of Death Report. https://
   wisqars.cdc.gov/data/lcd/home.
4. CDC WISQARS Leading Causes of Death Report. https://
   wisqars.cdc.gov/data/lcd/home
5. https://www.ncbi.nlm.nih.gov/pmc/articles
   /PMC9375853/
6. https://afsp.org/suicide-statistics
7. www.ncbi.nlm.nih.gov/pmc/articles/PMC9375853/
8. https://psychcentral.com/depression/teenage-depression
   -facts
9. https://www.ncbi.nlm.nih.gov/pmc/articles
   /PMC9375853/
10. https://ripplematch.com/journal/article/companies
    -that-prioritize-the-mental-health-of-their-employees
    -ebec5754/

CHAPTER 4

1. https://news.ohsu.edu/2017/05/11/women-responsible -for-most-health-decisions-in-the-home
2. http://offers.indeed.com/rs/699-SXJ-715/images /InteractiveResearch_ExecutiveSummary.pdf
3. https://www.forbes.com/sites/ryancraig/2019/06/07/top -employers-are-looking-for-talent-in-all-the-wrong -places/
4. https://www.forbes.com/sites/ryancraig/2019/06/07 /top-employers-are-looking-for-talent-in-all-the-wrong -places/
5. https://drugstorenews.com/news/cvs-jvs-open-learning -center-help-disadvantaged
6. https://cvshealth.com/news-and-insights/articles /developing-our-diverse-workforce

CHAPTER 5

1. https://www.forbes.com/sites/ellevate/2020/04/08/take -this-one-easy-step-to-conquer-self-doubt/
2. https://hbr.org/2020/11/how-to-actually-encourage -employee-accountability

CHAPTER 6

1. https://www.health.harvard.edu/mind-and-mood /exercise-can-boost-your-memory-and-thinking-skills

CHAPTER 7

1. https://www.kff.org/medicaid/issue-brief/10-things-to -know-about-medicaid-setting-the-facts-straight/

CHAPTER 8

1. https://www.5wpr.com/new/research/consumer-culture -report/
2. https://www.courant.com/news/orlando-nightclub -shooting/hc-orlando-aetna-employees-victims-0615 -20160614-story.html

CHAPTER 9
1. https://www.nationalgeographic.com/science/article
   /experts-warned-pandemic-decades-ago-why-not-ready
   -for-coronavirus

CHAPTER 10
1. https://fortune.com/company/cvs-health/fortune500/
2. https://www.cdc.gov/chronicdisease/healthequity/index
   .htm

INDEX

ABOUT THE AUTHOR

Karen S. Lynch is president and chief executive officer of CVS Health®, a Fortune 10 leading health solutions company, leading more than 300,000 purpose-driven colleagues toward delivering superior healthcare experiences for consumers while improving health, broadening access to care, and lowering costs.

Under Karen's leadership, CVS Health touches the lives of more than 100 million people through its healthcare benefits and pharmacy benefits management businesses, and presence in over 9,000 community health destinations across the United States.

Prior to becoming president and chief executive officer in February 2021, Karen was executive vice president of CVS Health and president of Aetna®, where she was responsible for delivering consumer-centric, holistic health care to the millions of people Aetna serves.

Karen was selected for the 2023 TIME100 annual list of the hundred most influential people in the world. She was named the top-ranking leader in 2021, 2022, and 2023 on the *Fortune* list of the "50 Most Powerful Women in Business." In 2022, *Fortune* named Karen the Most Inspirational CEO. She was also included on the Bloomberg

50 list of people who have changed global business. Karen is a member of the President of the United States Export Council. She was a former board member of U.S. Bancorp. She serves on the boards of America's Health Insurance Plans, the John F. Kennedy Library Foundation, and is an advisory board member for the Quell Foundation.

She is a graduate of Boston College and Boston University's Questrom School of Business. Karen lives in Florida with her husband, Kevin, and their dog, Piper. She is an avid runner and cyclist, and loves spending time with her grandson, Michael.